Healthy Cooking for Diabetics

Healthy Cooking for

Diabetics

60 Delicious and Natural Recipes for a Diabetic Diet

Contents

Introduction

If you have been diagnosed with diabetes—or someone close to you has—it can be particularly upsetting. However, major advances in our understanding of this condition and in its treatment and management mean that today "everything is possible" in life, even if you are diabetic. While it is important to keep a careful watch on your food intake—especially for people with type 1 diabetes and others who need to use insulin—there truly is still a whole world of delicious food out there for you to enjoy.

In recent years, health professionals have realized that it is not necessary for diabetics to eat as restricted a diet as once thought, nor is it necessary for them to forgo eating the same meals as the rest of their family and friends. The diet suitable for the majority of diabetics is one that everyone can enjoy—a healthy, nutritious diet with no food groups excluded and with no obscure, hard-to-find ingredients. The diabetic diet is, in fact, a great way to eat for anyone who values their health—and their taste buds! Just a glance through these pages will give you a taste of the fantastic recipes that you, your friends, and your family can feast on.

Types of Diabetes

Type 1 Diabetes

Type 1 diabetes is most commonly diagnosed in childhood (and used to be known as "juvenile diabetes" for that reason) but it can actually begin at any age. It is also called "insulin-dependent diabetes" because, for those with type 1 diabetes, insulin is vital in its management.

Insulin is a hormone that helps your body use the glucose your body gets through the food you eat, providing you with energy. In type 1 diabetes, the body is unable to produce any insulin, so glucose builds up in the blood. Meanwhile, your body begins to look for sources of energy elsewhere and breaks down its fat stores or the proteins in your muscles—which is why people with the disease can lose weight.

The causes are still being researched, but type 1 diabetes may be triggered by viruses or bacterial infections. Apart from weight loss, other usual symptoms include having to urinate more frequently (because the body is trying to flush out the unused, surplus glucose) and extreme tiredness. Currently, there is no cure for type 1 diabetes, but it can be treated and managed using insulin injections or an insulin pump in conjunction with a healthy lifestyle and diet.

Type 2 Diabetes

Accounting for 90 percent of diabetes cases, type 2 diabetes is the most common type of diabetes. It develops when the body doesn't produce enough insulin, or when the insulin that is produced doesn't work properly (called "insulin resistance").

Type 2 diabetes used to be called "midlife onset diabetes," because it does, indeed, affect a large number of people in midlife, but there are growing numbers of younger people with the condition. Many experts link this surge to an increase in obesity and inactivity. High blood pressure and a large waist circumference (because fat stored around the midriff, known as "visceral fat," appears to decrease insulin sensitivity and increase insulin resistance) are two risk factors.

Type 2 diabetes can cause serious long-term health problems, so it is important to be diagnosed early and control your blood glucose levels to prevent these complications. Blood sugar levels may be controlled with a healthy diet, weight loss, if necessary, and increased physical activity, although sometimes treatment with medication and/or insulin is also needed.

Gestational Diabetes

This type of diabetes occurs for the first time in women during pregnancy and, in most cases, disappears after pregnancy is over. The cause is usually that the pregnant woman has a much higher than normal level of glucose in her blood and can't produce enough insulin to make her body able to use it all. It can be managed and treated in a similar way to type 2 diabetes.

What Is a Healthy Diet for Diabetics?

A healthy diet is important for everyone, but it is especially important for diabetics. Across the world over the past sixty or so years, health professionals and researchers have wavered somewhat about what constitutes the best diet for diabetics. A recent report by the American Diabetes Association stated, "There is one certainty about diet and diabetes—there is no one diet that is right for all."

Of course, research into the "best" diet for diabetics is still ongoing, and there are one or two areas that may turn out to be exciting. For example, there has been much debate in the past few years about higher-protein, moderate-carbohydrate diets. Some research shows that such a diet can help control blood insulin even better than the higher-carbohydrate diet that was once usually recommended, and is better in helping with weight loss and weight control. There is also interest in a diet high in "resistant starch"—a type of dietary fiber naturally found in many carbohydrate-rich foods, such as potatoes, grains, and beans, particularly when these foods are cooked and then cooled. It gets its name because it "resists" digestion, and it appears to increase the body's ability to burn fat, reduce overall hunger, and improve blood sugar control.

At the present time, however, the recommendations given by leading diabetes organizations for how diabetics should eat are strikingly similar to the guidelines that nondiabetics are often asked to follow for a generally healthy diet. Basically, we all need a good balance of the major nutrients ("macronutrients")—carbohydrates, fats, and protein—in our diets.

Carbohydrates

Carbohydrates are our body's main energy source. Carbohydrates—including both starches and sugars—easily convert into glucose within the digestive system, which is then used to provide us with the energy we need in our daily lives. Some good sources of carbohydrates for diabetics include legumes (such as beans, peas, and lentils), whole grains (such as oats, barley, rye, spelt, rice, and wheat), and starchy vegetables (including root vegetables) and whole fruits, particularly those with a lower glycemic index (see panel, opposite page). It is important to eat enough—but not too many—carbohydrates, because they can't be stored in the body, so they are instead converted into body fat.

Fats

Fats have many roles within the body, and the fats we eat in food are broken down into fatty acids of many different types. These help proteins to do their work, assist our bodies in storing and using certain vitamins, and also aid in the control of growth, immune function, reproduction, and metabolism.

Although fat is energy dense and easily stored in the body, there is no need for diabetics to avoid eating fat. Indeed, some fats—monounsaturated fats (found in good quantities in some foods, such as olive oil, avocados, and some nuts and seeds) and certain types of polyunsaturated fats (found in good quantities in foods such as oily fish, some nuts and seeds, and plant oils) have positive health benefits for everyone, including diabetics. Saturated fats (found in large quantities in foods such as whole dairy produce, fatty cuts of meat, and many highly processed foods, such as pastries, desserts, cakes, and cookies) are less beneficial and, if eaten in large quantities, may increase the risk of health problems, including cardiovascular disease. Hydrogenated fats—fats altered in the manufacturing process to harden them—are thought to be even worse for the health than saturated fats and are best avoided. These fats are slowly being phased out from food manufacturing, so it is becoming easier to find products free from hydrogenated fats.

Protein

Like fats, protein has many roles to play—our connective tissue, skin, hair, and muscles are all made up of protein, and without it we couldn't maintain our muscle mass, our vital organs, and our skin, or build new cells. Protein plays a crucial role in all of our cells, including our DNA, hormones, and enzymes. All these functions need us to eat protein regularly. A diet containing adequate protein is equally important to diabetics as it is to nondiabetics, as long as there is a balance of sources—not relying on too much red meat, for example. Good protein sources for diabetics include fish, poultry, small amounts of lean red meat, legumes, eggs, reduced-fat dairy produce, and nuts and seeds.

The Glycemic Index

The glycemic index is a ranking of all carbohydrate foods according to the rate at which the starches and sugars they contain are absorbed into the body and get into the bloodstream as blood glucose. A ranking of 100 is the highest, while a ranking of 1 is the lowest. Foods with a high GI (over 70) are the quickest to be absorbed and foods with a low GI (55 or under) are the slowest to be absorbed. Medium GI foods have a rating of 56 to 69. The glycemic index was originally devised in the 1980s to help diabetics to make wise food choices, and thus help them to control their blood sugars and medications.

In practice, however, most people eat or drink high-carbohydrate, high-GI foods along with other foods. For example, you may have boiled potatoes with fish, or pasta with a cheese and ham sauce. The fat and protein accompanying your carbohydrate food can reduce the "spike" effect. As a result, it may be important for diabetics to eat carbohydrate foods—particularly those at the high end of the GI ranking—with proteins and fats to minimize this effect. (The glycemic index lists only carbohydrate foods; there is no GI ranking for proteins and fats.) Most studies have also shown that, compared to low-GI meals, high-GI meals lead to lower satiety and increased hunger levels or increased food intake, so eating more low-GI foods can be useful for weight-loss diets. Finally, the glycemic effect of a food also depends on how much of it you eat. The glycemic load (GL) of a food or meal calculates the effect by using a formula based on the weights of carbohydrate foods consumed as well as their theoretical GI value.

High-GI foods include: Sugar of all types, watermelon, bananas, mashed potatoes, white bread, and cornflakes.

Medium-GI foods include: Sweet potatoes, boiled potatoes, pasta, corn, oatmeal, whole-grain bread, oranges, grapes, and figs.

Low-GI foods include: Lentils, kidney beans, chickpeas, baked beans, whole barley, apples, dried apricots, plums, cherries, plain yogurt, and milk.

Foods to Avoid

So, are there any types of food that diabetics should avoid? The answer to that question is "no"—or "not completely." Diabetes organizations recommend keeping your **saturated fat** intake low, but there are no current guidelines on maximum intake specific to diabetics. Because of the link between cardiovascular disease, high blood pressure, and diabetes, it is wise to limit your **sodium** intake to a maximum of 1,500 milligrams a day—not just of added salt but also of high-sodium foods, such as bacon and ham, prepared soups, sauces, and bouillon cubes, and takeout food. Moderate amounts of **alcohol**—no more than one small alcoholic drink a day for women and two for men—are fine (but first consult your physician). Intake of **carbohydrates** in their simple, highly processed forms (such as sugar, white flour, white pasta, white rice, and goodies, such as commercial pastries, cakes, and cookies) needs to be watched. This is really important if you are overweight, because these types of foods tend to be low in nutrients and high in calories and sometimes fat.

Sugar—What You Need to Know

Dietitians divide the sugars that we eat into two different types—intrinsic (the sugars that form a natural part of the structure of a food, as in fruits, for example) and extrinsic (those that are not a natural part of a food and instead are added in the manufacturing process or at the table). Milk contains an extrinsic sugar, lactose, which is not normally grouped with the extrinsic sugars. Extrinsic sugars may also be referred to as "free sugars."

* **High intrinsic sugar** foods include many fruits, especially dried and tropical fruits, and a surprising number of vegetables, such as beets, carrots, corn, bell peppers, potatoes, peas, onions, and parsnips. However, it is important not to avoid all fruits and vegetables containing sugar, because they provide a range of important nutrients as well as dietary fiber and health-promoting plant compounds.

* **High or very high extrinsic sugar** foods include confectionery, cakes, desserts, soft drinks, and cookies, as well as some breakfast cereals and bars, low-fat fruit yogurts, and some alcoholic drinks, such as sweet wine.

So if you are cutting back on sugar, should you use sugar substitutes instead? There are many different types:

* **Natural sugar alternatives—**these include maple syrup, agave nectar, date syrup, and rice malt syrup and are useful as an occasional, and often flavorsome, alternative to sugar. They have similar calorie contents to sugar but tend to be higher in fructose (fruit sugar). The American Diabetes Association says agave nectar and other natural sweeteners should be limited in a diabetic diet and the consensus seems to be that they offer little benefit over sugar.

* **Artificial sweeteners—**these include all zero-calorie and extremely low-calorie sugar substitutes, such as aspartame, saccharin, acesulfame-K, and sucralose. All these have been passed as safe in the United States and don't affect the blood sugar. However, some people find they leave an aftertaste or simply do not taste as good as sugar.

* **Sugar alcohols—**these products include mannitol, sorbitol, erythritol, and xylitol and contain fewer calories than sugar—about half to one-third less. Sugar alcohols can cause diarrhea, bloating, and weight gain if consumed in large quantities and do affect blood sugars.

* **Stevia—**a unique sweetener, stevia is made with an approved extract from a plant, Stevia rebaudiana, native to South America. Recent research shows it may help to reduce high blood pressure, maintain constant blood sugar levels, and minimize liver and kidney damage in diabetics. There are many different brands and varieties of stevia sweetener available—we've used both granulated stevia (the calorie-free version that can be used to replace sugar teaspoon for teaspoon) and liquid stevia.

Reading Labels

When you buy processed foods, be aware that sugar can be disguised in the ingredients labels in a variety of different names. All of the following are basically types of sugar: *cane sugar, corn sweetener, corn syrup, corn syrup solids, dextrose, fructose, fruit juice concentrates, honey, lactose, maltose, malt syrup, and maple syrup.*

Healthy Eating for Diabetics—Top Ten Tips

1. Choose a wide variety of foods

This will help to make sure you get all the nutrients that your body needs in a good balance.

2. Try to eat naturally

Keep highly processed items, such as store-bought cakes, pies, cookies, and so on, for occasional consumption. Eating a natural diet is an easy way to reduce your intake of saturated and hydrogenated fats, sodium, and sugar.

3. Choose fruit for a sweet taste

For those with a sweet tooth, low-GI fresh fruits, such as cherries, plums, apples, and peaches, are an ideal easy dessert—their fiber content slows down insulin release.

4. Limit soft drinks and juices

High-sugar drinks, such as colas and other soft drinks and fruit juice, are digested especially quickly and can provoke high blood sugar.

5. Choose water

The best drinks to choose are water, or tea or coffee with a little skim or low-fat milk, if desired, all of which have minimal effect on blood sugar.

6. Eat regularly

This is especially important for type 1 diabetics and helps to prevent hypoglycemia (low blood sugar). Eating regularly also helps to avoid hunger pangs and may help to control weight.

7. Think "good" carbohydrates every day

Eat carbohydrates with a high fiber content and/or a low GI and/or a high content of resistant starch (see page 7)—they can also be a great source of nutrients.

8. Make your plates colorful

Foods that are green, orange, yellow, red, or purple, for example, tend to contain high levels of antioxidant compounds, which can help to prevent diabetes-related diseases, such as cardiovascular disease.

9. Take healthy snacks with you

When out and about, carry portable snacks, such as nuts mixed with a few dried apricots and raisins; they are ideal for short-term and long-term energy and stable blood sugar.

10. Take time over your food

Don't forget to enjoy preparing your food and eating it. Food is a pleasure to be savored and can even help you to reverse your diabetes symptoms.

Daily Nutritional Guidelines

The recipes in this book have been developed to fit into what is generally considered to be a healthy diet for both diabetics and nondiabetics, while also focusing on the "good" carbohydrates and keeping added (extrinsic) sugar to a minimum. We have assumed that 50 percent of total daily calories will come from carbohydrates (to consist of mainly low-GI carbohydrates high in fiber and/or resistant starch); a maximum of 30 percent from fat (of which no more than one-third should be saturated fat), and 20 percent from protein (which should be eaten mostly in the form of the proteins described on page 8 as being best for diabetics). However, protein intake is flexible and could vary between 10 and 25 percent, depending on individual preference (adjusting proportions of carbohydrates/fat accordingly). Advice on sugar intake varies across the world, but we have based our guidelines on a total sugar intake equivalent to or less than 10 percent of daily calories, most of which should come from intrinsic sugars.

The table below shows how this advice translates into a nutritional breakdown for each meal of the day. The information in this table is based on a daily intake of 2,000 calories, which is suitable for the weight maintenance of an average woman.

	Calories (cal)	Maximum carbs	Maximum total sugars	of which extrinsic sugars	Maximum total fat	of which maximum saturated fats	Protein
Breakfast	400	53 g	10 g	5 g	13 g	4.5 g	10–25 g
Lunch	500	67 g	10 g	0 g	17 g	5.5 g	12.5–31 g
Dinner	600	80 g	10 g	0 g	20 g	6.5 g	15–38 g
Snack or side	200	27 g	5 g	0 g	7 g	2 g	5–12.5 g
Dessert or bake	200	27 g	10 g	5 g	7 g	2 g	5–12.5 g
Milk allowance (3½ fluid ounces low-fat milk)	50	5 g	5 g	0 g	2 g	1.2 g	3.3 g
Daily total	1,950*	259 g	50 g	10 g	66 g	21.7 g	50.8–122.3 g

* With an additional maximum 50 calories for "free" extras, such as green vegetables and salad, taking total to 2,000 calories

The above values are intended as only a guideline. Although people with type 2 diabetes do not need to work out every gram of carbohydrate or sugar in every meal, those with type 1 diabetes will need to match their insulin intake with their carbohydrate intake. It is important that all individuals consult the health care professional or team monitoring their diabetes before making any dietary changes.

In order to be sure of a good variety of recipes in this book, the exact nutritional breakdowns of the individual recipes vary in terms of the proportions of macronutrients they contain. It is therefore important to balance these across the day's eating. For example, if you choose a low-protein (or low-carbohydrate) lunch, you should then pick a higher-protein (or high-carbohydrate) dinner and vice versa.

In the pages that follow, we give two seven-day diet plans as examples of how to build a day's healthy eating based on the recipes in this book. Plan 1 is designed to help those with a healthy body weight maintain that weight, while Plan 2 targets weight loss. According to the International Diabetes Federation, 80 percent of the world's type 2 diabetics are overweight or obese at the time of diagnosis. Reducing body weight by just 5–10 percent can help to slow or stop the progress of type 2 diabetes, so losing weight is a positive step that people with the disease can take to manage their health.

Diet Plans

Plan 1: **Weight Maintenance**

* **Calorie goal:** approximately 2,000 calories a day (based on average adult woman). Men should aim for approximately 2,500 calories a day and, therefore, increase portion sizes throughout by 25 percent.

* **Consume freely:** Leafy green vegetables and salad vegetables (such as lettuce, cucumber, radish, and celery), fresh herbs and spices, lemon juice, and vinegar.

* **To drink:** Water, or tea or coffee (with milk from allowance).

* **Milk allowance:** 3½ fluid ounces, or scant ½ cup, low-fat milk (50 calories) for use in tea and coffee, or as you prefer. (Daily totals all include milk allowance.)

* **Alcohol:** No more than one small alcoholic drink a day for women and two for men (on consultation with your health care professional). Calories to be taken from dessert allowance.

	Recipe/Food	Calories
Day one	**Total (including milk allowance)**	**1,931**
Breakfast	*Coconut and blackberry oatmeal* (p. 21)	322
Midmorning snack	*Nut and seed bar* (p. 141)	213
	1 satsuma	40
Lunch	*Eggplant paprika salad* (p. 68)	475
	1 apple	60
Dinner	*Chicken scallops with cherry tomatoes* (p. 88)	342
	Sweet potato fries (p. 112)	183
Dessert	*Individual plum and rhubarb crisp* (p. 150)	208
	3½ tbsp. Greek-style yogurt	38
Day two	**Total (including milk allowance)**	**1,991**
Breakfast	*Eggs Benedict with asparagus and prosciutto* (p. 36)	342
	1 kiwi	30
Midmorning snack	1 heaping tbsp. *Homemade cashew nut butter* (p. 128)	153
	2 dark rye crispbreads	68
Lunch	4½ oz. smoked salmon	275
	1 slice *Pumpernickel bread* (p. 137)	135
	2 tsp. dill mustard sauce	46
Dinner	*Spaghetti and meatballs* (p. 83)	585
	1 oz. Parmesan cheese shavings	116
	Large mixed leaf salad with 2 tsp. vinaigrette dressing	40
Dessert	*Vanilla custard cup with raspberry coulis* (p. 154)	151
Day three	**Total (including milk allowance)**	**1,997**
Breakfast	*Healthiest-ever muesli* (p. 22)	429
	1 chopped apple (skin included)	60
	⅔ cup unsweetened almond milk	20
Midmorning snack	1¼ oz. reduced-fat cheddar cheese	110
	2 thin, round seeded oat cakes	88
Lunch	*Spicy chickpea and red pepper soup* (p. 53)	366
	2 *Beet brownie bites* (p. 149)	148
	1 tbsp. Greek-style yogurt	17
Dinner	*Salmon ramen* (p. 101)	397
	⅓ cup brown long-grain rice, cooked	212
Snack	10 almonds and 4 walnut halves	100

Day four	**Total** (including milk allowance)	**1,898**
Breakfast	*Almond butter and raspberry smoothie* (p. 26)	338
	2 Brazil nuts	66
Midmorning snack	*Cheese and herb biscuit* (p. 138)	213
Lunch	*Pulled pork wrap* (p. 59)	467
	5 cherries	25
Dinner	*Tuna and broccoli pasta casserole* (p. 102)	533
	Large mixed leaf salad with 1 tbsp. vinaigrette dressing	60
Dessert	⅔ cup raspberries	42
Snack	2 tsp. *Homemade cashew nut butter* (p. 128)	76
	1 whole-grain, seeded rice cake	28
Day five	**Total** (including milk allowance)	**1,973**
Breakfast	*Carrot cake muffin* (p. 33)	318
	⅔ cup blackberries	43
Midmorning snack	*Cannellini bean dip with crudités* (p. 124)	184
Lunch	*Rib eye steak salad with arugula and Parmesan* (p. 71)	413
	⅓ cup almonds and 2 dried apricots	193
Dinner	*Chicken and shrimp jambalaya* (p. 94)	548
Dessert	*Berry and bread pudding* (p. 153)	224
Day six	**Total** (including milk allowance)	**1,946**
Breakfast	*Potato pancakes with smoked salmon* (p. 44)	353
	1 orange	60
Midmorning snack	1 heaping tbsp. *Homemade cashew nut butter* (p. 128)	153
	1 dark rye crispbread	34
Lunch	Avocado, tomato, and mozzarella salad: ½ small sliced avocado and 1 sliced tomato topped with 2¾ oz. torn buffalo mozzarella, drizzled with balsamic vinegar and seasoned with salt and pepper	435
	2 dark rye crispbreads	68
Dinner	*Winter root vegetable casserole* (p. 108)	458
	¼ cup walnuts	164
Dessert	⅔ cup raspberries	39
	¾ oz melted or grated semisweet chocolate	120
Day seven	**Total** (including milk allowance)	**1,928**
Breakfast	1½ heaping tbsp. *Homemade cashew nut butter* (p. 128)	230
	1 slice *Pumpernickel bread* (p. 137)	135
	½ pink or red grapefruit	42
Midmorning snack	*Cheese and herb biscuit* (p. 138)	213
Lunch	*Smoked mackerel, beet, and new potato salad* (p. 72)	435
	2 dark rye crispbreads	68
Dinner	*Chili con carne* (p. 80)	622
Dessert	1 very small banana and 5 blueberries	76
	⅓ cup fat-free Greek-style yogurt	57

Plan 2: Weight Loss

* **Calorie goal:** approximately 1,500 calories a day (based on average adult woman). Men should aim for approximately 2,000 calories a day and, therefore, increase portion sizes throughout by 33 percent.

* **Consume freely:** Leafy green vegetables and salad vegetables (such as lettuce, cucumber, radish, and celery), fresh herbs and spices, lemon juice, and vinegar.

* **To drink:** water, or tea or coffee (with milk from allowance). Avoid alcohol.

* **Milk allowance:** 3½ fluid ounces, or scant ½ cup low-fat milk (50 calories) for use in tea and coffee, or as you prefer. (Daily totals all include milk allowance.)

	Recipe/Food	Calories
Day one	**Total (including milk allowance)**	**1,535**
Breakfast	*Spinach scramble with toasted rye bread* (p. 40)	247
	½ pink grapefruit	42
Midmorning snack	*Mixed vegetable chips* (p. 127)	128
Lunch	*Mixed seafood chowder* (p. 54)	362
	1 small apple	53
Dinner	*Chinese marinated flank steak with noodles* (p. 84)	533
Dessert	*Fluffy lemon whip* (p. 156)	120
Day two	**Total (including milk allowance)**	**1,430**
Breakfast	Oatmeal: Simmer ½ cup rolled oats with 1 cup water, according to package directions, until thick and soft. Stir in 1½ tsp. milled flaxseed and top with ¼ cup low-fat milk	229
	⅓ cup raspberries	26
Midmorning snack	1 extra-large hard-boiled egg, 1 dark rye crispbread, and 4 cherry tomatoes	154
Lunch	*Split pea and ham soup* (p. 50)	315
	1 (1-oz.) slice whole-grain bread	70
Dinner	*Monkfish, mushroom, and red pepper skewer* (p. 99)	429
	Large mixed leaf and cucumber salad with 2 tsp. balsamic vinegar	9
Dessert	2 *Beet brownie bites* (p. 149)	74
Day three	**Total (including milk allowance)**	**1,419**
Breakfast	*Nutty yogurt and melon sundae* (p. 24)	172
	1 slice *Pumpernickel bread*, toasted (p. 137)	135
	2 tsp. extra-light spread	10
Midmorning snack	*Oat, blueberry, and nut cookie* (p. 142)	145
Lunch	*Avocado, artichoke, and almond salad* (p. 67)	364
Dinner	*Chicken chow mein* (p. 93)	469
Dessert	1 *Beet brownie bite* (p. 149)	74

Day four	Total (including milk allowance)	1,446
Breakfast	*Rustic blueberry, lemon, and seed scone* (p. 30)	199
	1 small apple	53
Midmorning snack	2 ½ tbsp./1 oz. *Fruit, nut, and seed trail mix* (p. 130)	132
Lunch	*Mini pizza muffin* (p. 56)	367
	Large mixed leaf salad with 2 tsp. vinaigrette dressing	40
Dinner	*Breaded fish with chunky fries* (p. 96)	412
Dessert	*Vanilla custard cup with raspberry coulis* (p. 154)	151
	⅔ cup raspberries	42
Day five	**Total (including milk allowance)**	**1,489**
Breakfast	*Poached egg in tomato sauce* (p. 38)	312
Midmorning snack	1 dark rye crispbread	34
	2 tsp. *Homemade cashew nut butter* (p. 128)	76
Lunch	*Chicken and corn burrito* (p. 60)	361
	6 almonds	34
Dinner	*Butternut squash and spinach curry* (p. 106)	486
	1 tsp. mango chutney	16
Dessert	¾ oz. semisweet chocolate	120
Day six	**Total (including milk allowance)**	**1,453**
Breakfast	*Crepes with creamy citrus filling* (p. 29)	316
Midmorning snack	½ oz. reduced-fat cheddar cheese	47
	1 thin, round seeded oat cake	44
Lunch	*Lentil and tuna salad* (p. 75)	225
	1 slice *Pumpernickel bread* (p. 137)	135
	1 plum	30
Dinner	5½ oz. hot-smoked salmon fillet	312
	5½ oz. new potatoes, steamed with skins on and cooled	104
	¾ cup green beans and 1 cup broccoli, steamed	50
	Juice of ¼ lemon	0
	1 tsp. butter	36
Dessert	¼ cup ricotta cheese with 2 tsp. granulated stevia	82
	⅓ cup blackberries	22
Day seven	**Total (including milk allowance)**	**1,454**
Breakfast	*Turkey sausage patties with mushrooms and tomatoes* (p. 43)	239
	1 (1-oz.) slice whole-grain bread	70
Midmorning snack	10 almonds and 4 walnut halves	98
Lunch	*Crustless zucchini and fava bean quiche* (p. 64)	412
Dinner	*Lentil burger* (p. 105)	363
	Red cabbage, orange, and walnut coleslaw (p. 120)	148
Dessert	Scant ½ cup fat-free Greek-style yogurt	57
	¼ cup blueberries	17

Breakfasts

1
2
2

Coconut and Blackberry Oatmeal

Oatmeal is an ideal breakfast for controlling blood sugar, and the coconut and berries make it even more healthy and delicious.

Calories 322 // Carbohydrates 38.7 g // Sugars 9.9 g // Protein 10.6 g // Fiber 7.3 g // Fat 15.2 g // Saturated fat 4.1 g // Sodium 520 mg

1 cup coconut water
1 cup water
1 cup skim milk
1¾ cups rolled oats
½ teaspoon ground allspice
1 teaspoon salt
2 teaspoons granulated stevia
⅓ cup low-fat plain yogurt

To Serve
⅔ cup blackberries
½ cup chopped hazelnuts
¼ cup dry unsweetened coconut

1. Put the coconut water, water, and milk into a saucepan and stir well to combine.

2. Stir in the oats, allspice, salt, stevia, and yogurt and bring to a simmer. Reduce the heat and gently simmer, stirring frequently, for 10 minutes, or until the oatmeal is thick and creamy and the oats are tender.

3. Transfer to serving dishes. Top with the blackberries and sprinkle with the chopped hazelnuts and dry coconut. Serve immediately.

Serves: 4 // Preparation time: 10 minutes // Cooking time: 15 minutes

Natural leaf-base stevia is a healthy alternative sweetener to sugar or artificial sweeteners (see page 11). It is calorie-free with no effect on blood sugar. You can buy it in granulated or liquid form from most supermarkets.

Healthiest-Ever Muesli

Most store-bought muesli and granolas contain high levels of dried fruit, so they are high in sugars. This version contains a healthier level of sugar.

Calories 429 // Carbohydrates 53.5 g // Sugars 5.6 g // Protein 14.0 g // Fiber 10.9 g // Fat 20.2 g // Saturated fat 3.0 g // Sodium Trace

Milled flaxseed is readily available in supermarkets. The milling process means the nutrients in the ground seeds are much better absorbed than those in whole seeds, which tend to pass through the digestive system whole.

3 cups oat flakes
¾ cup rye flakes
⅓ cup walnuts
12 Brazil nuts
1 tablespoon sunflower seeds
1 tablespoon pumpkin seeds
2 tablespoons raisins
2 tablespoons chopped dried apricots
2 tablespoons milled flaxseed

1. In a mixing bowl, thoroughly combine the oat flakes and rye flakes.

2. Chop the walnuts and Brazil nuts and add to the flakes with the sunflower seeds, pumpkin seeds, and raisins.

3. Mix the dried apricots with the milled flaxseed—the seed meal will coat the apricots and prevent them from sticking together. Stir into the muesli.

4. Store in an airtight container if not using immediately. You can easily double or triple the quantity and store in the refrigerator for one week.

Serves: 4 // Preparation time: 10 minutes // Cooking time: None

Nutty Yogurt and Melon Sundaes

Colorful and tempting, this refreshing breakfast is a perfect start to the day when you feel like something light.

Calories 172 / / Carbohydrates 14.2 g / / Sugars 10.0 g / / Protein 12.0 g / / Fiber 2.1 g / / Fat 8.3 g / / Saturated fat 1.3 g / / Sodium 80 mg

Similar in texture to mascarpone but with no fat, no added sugar, and a great protein content, quark is a good addition to your diet. Just 3½ ounces contains nearly your whole daily requirement of calcium.

¾ cup low-fat yogurt
¾ cup low-fat cream cheese or quark
1 teaspoon granulated stevia
¼ cup pistachio nuts, coarsely chopped
⅓ cup toasted slivered almonds
1⅓ cups diced watermelon
3 tablespoons pomegranate seeds

1. In a mixing bowl, thoroughly combine the yogurt, cream cheese, and stevia.

2. Stir in half the pistachio nuts and slivered almonds.

3. Divide the diced watermelon among four serving glasses and spoon one-quarter of the yogurt mixture over the top of each.

4. Sprinkle with the remaining nuts, followed by the pomegranate seeds, and serve the sundaes immediately.

Serves: 4 / / Preparation time: 10 minutes / / Cooking time: None

1
2
3

Almond Butter and Raspberry Smoothies

If you don't usually eat breakfast, try this smoothie. It is a really quick and tasty breakfast that is packed with nutrients.

Calories 338 / / Carbohydrates 28.4 g / / Sugars 10.6 g / / Protein 6.7 g / / Fiber 10.7 g / / Fat 14.1 g / / Saturated fat 1.0 g / / Sodium 80 mg

Bananas are a rich source of potassium and resistant starch, both of which have benefits for diabetics. Potassium appears to help to regulate the production of insulin, while resistant starch increases insulin sensitivity.

1 banana
1⅔ cups raspberries
1¾ cups unsweetened almond milk
2½ tablespoons almond butter
4 teaspoons granulated stevia
2 teaspoons vanilla extract
ice cubes

1. Peel the banana and put into a blender with the raspberries.

2. Add the almond milk, almond butter, stevia, and vanilla extract. Fill up with ice cubes.

3. Blend until smooth. Drink immediately or store in the refrigerator overnight.

Serves: 2 / / Preparation time: 10 minutes / / Cooking time: None

1
2
3

1
2
4

Crepes with Creamy Citrus Filling

This breakfast has a great balance of protein, carbohydrates, and fat. The rye and spelt flours give the crepes a nutty, slightly sweet taste.

Calories 316 / / Carbohydrates 35.8 g / / Sugars 9.1 g / / Protein 19.7 g / / Fiber 3.4 g / / Fat 10.7 g / / Saturated fat 4.3 g / / Sodium 640 mg

1 cup ricotta cheese
¾ cup fat-free Greek-style yogurt
1 tablespoon grated orange zest
2 tablespoons orange juice
1–2 teaspoons granulated stevia
⅓ cup plus 1 tablespoon rye flour
⅓ cup spelt flour or whole-wheat flour
⅓ cup all-purpose flour
1 teaspoon salt
2 medium eggs
1 tablespoon peanut oil
⅔ cup skim milk
½ cup water
cooking spray, for oiling
1 orange, peeled, segmented, and chopped
2 teaspoons confectioners' sugar, for dusting

1. In a bowl, combine the ricotta, yogurt, orange zest, orange juice, and stevia. Set aside in the refrigerator until ready to serve.

2. In a mixing bowl, stir together the rye flour, spelt flour, all-purpose flour, and salt, then whisk in the eggs, oil, milk, and water until completely smooth.

3. Heat a small, nonstick skillet over medium-high heat and coat with cooking spray.

4. When the pan is hot, pour in one-quarter of the batter and swirl it around to coat the pan. Cook for 1 minute, or until the underside is golden, then flip the crepe over with a spatula and cook for 1 minute on the other side. Transfer the cooked crepe to a warm plate while you cook the remaining batter.

5. Repeat to make three more crepes, spraying the pan between each addition. (You could make eight mini crepes, if you prefer.)

6. Place the crepes on serving plates, then fill with the ricotta mixture and a little of the chopped orange and fold over. Decorate with the remaining chopped orange and dust with confectioners' sugar.

Serves: 4 / / Preparation time: 20 minutes / / Cooking time: 10 minutes

Spelt is an ancient cousin of modern wheat that is enjoying a revival today and is available both as flour and whole grains. Because it contains more fat and protein than wheat, it has a useful lower GI rating.

Rustic Blueberry, Lemon, and Seed Scones

These unique, rustic-looking scones are made using a tasty, nutrient-rich seeded flour, as well as flaxseed and blueberries.

Calories 199 / / Carbohydrates 25.9 g / / Sugars 3.8 g / / Protein 6.0 g / / Fiber 2.9 g / / Fat 7.3 g / / Saturated fat 1.4 g / / Sodium 480 mg

cooking spray, for oiling
2¼ cups whole-wheat seeded flour, plus extra for dusting
1 cup oats
1½ tablespoons milled flaxseed
2 teaspoons baking powder
½ teaspoon baking soda
1 teaspoon salt
3 heaping tablespoons granulated stevia
¾ cup small blueberries
grated zest of 1 lemon
1 cup low-fat plain yogurt
2 tablespoons peanut oil
juice of ½ lemon
½ cup skim milk
½ cup reduced-fat sunflower spread, to serve

1. Preheat the oven to 400°F. Spray a baking sheet with cooking spray.

2. Put the flour, oats, milled flaxseed, baking powder, baking soda, salt, and stevia into a large mixing bowl and thoroughly combine with a fork. Stir in the blueberries and lemon zest.

3. Put the yogurt, oil, lemon juice, and milk into a small bowl and whisk together.

4. Pour the yogurt mixture into the flour mixture and stir until you have a coarse dough.

5. Flour your hands and divide the mixture into 12 coarse balls and place on the prepared baking sheet. Bake in the preheated oven for 15 minutes, or until the scones are golden and firm.

6. Let cool for 10 minutes, then spread each scone with 2 teaspoons sunflower spread and eat warm or cold. The scones can be stored in an airtight container for one or two days, or can be frozen in a freezer-proof plastic bag for up to one month.

Makes: 12 / / Preparation time: 20–25 minutes / / Cooking time: 15 minutes, plus cooling

Plain yogurt is a great ingredient to use in baking for diabetics because it has a low GI rating of just 14. Other ingredients that bring down the glycemic load of these scones are the seeds, oats, blueberries, and oil.

1
2
5

1

3

5

Carrot Cake Muffins

These delicious carrot, raisin, and walnut muffins are surprisingly low in sugar and fat, and are packed with fiber and vitamin A-rich carrots.

Calories 318 / / Carbohydrates 47.0 g / / Sugars 9.0 g / / Protein 9.0 g / / Fiber 7.9 g / / Fat 12.5 g / / Saturated fat 4.2 g / / Sodium 400 mg

3¾ cups whole-wheat flour
1 teaspoon baking soda
1 teaspoon baking powder
½ teaspoon salt
1 teaspoon ground cinnamon
¼ teaspoon ground ginger
2 tablespoons canola oil
1 egg
2 egg whites
3 tablespoons granulated stevia
2 teaspoons vanilla extract
½ cup unsweetened applesauce
⅓ cup unsweetened almond milk
8 carrots (about 1 pound)
½ cup raisins
½ cup chopped walnuts
¾ cup dry unsweetened coconut

1. Preheat the oven to 350°F. Line ten sections in a 12-cup muffin pan with muffin cups.

2. Sift together the flour, baking soda, baking powder, salt, cinnamon, and ginger into a bowl, adding any bran left in the sifter.

3. Beat together the oil, egg, egg whites, stevia, and vanilla extract in a bowl until creamy, then stir in the applesauce and almond milk.

4. Peel and grate the carrots, then add to the liquid ingredients with the raisins, walnuts, and half the dry coconut. Add the flour mixture, stirring until just combined.

5. Divide the batter among the muffin cups. Bake in the preheated oven for 25 minutes, or until a toothpick inserted into the center of a muffin comes out clean.

6. Let cool in the pan until cool enough to handle, then transfer to a wire rack to cool completely. Decorate with the remaining dry coconut or wrap in freezer-proof plastic bags and freeze for up to one month.

Makes: 10 / / Preparation time: 20–25 minutes / / Cooking time: 25 minutes, plus cooling

Almond milk is becoming very popular across the world as an alternative to cow milk. The unsweetened version contains just 0.1 percent sugar, compared to 5 percent sugar in dairy milk.

Building Activity into Your Day

If you are diabetic, or want to help prevent yourself from developing diabetes, the argument for getting moving is strong. Many studies across the world have found that activity is critical for optimum health in those with insulin resistance, prediabetes, type 2 diabetes, gestational diabetes, and diabetes-related health complications, such as poor bone health. Even moderate exercise improves insulin action and can assist with the management of blood glucose levels, lipids, blood pressure, and cardiovascular risk, as well as improving stress levels, sleep, and mood.

Ask your health care professional for help in deciding what is best for you, and then try our tips for building more activity into your everyday life.

* If you're currently mostly sedentary, you need to start gently—even simply getting up and standing more often (for example, when talking on the phone) is a good start.

* Small, manageable chunks of activity are usually the way to go after that. Everyday activities, such as walking up the stairs or inclines, dancing in the living room to the radio, or gardening will all help.

* Think about one extra activity you could try that would fit in well with your current lifestyle. For example, walking with added pleasure—with binoculars to spot birds, with a camera, or with a friend. If you sleep poorly, a 15-minute walk after dinner in the spring and summer months is ideal.

* If going to a gym is not for you—perhaps it's too expensive, doesn't fit in with your schedule, or is a long way to travel—you can buy inexpensive resistance bands or a basic rowing machine and do some exercise at home, even while you watch TV.

* Once or twice a day, try to get your heart rate up. This means you'll feel warm, perhaps break into a light sweat, and know your lungs are working harder. This could happen during everyday tasks, such as housework, car cleaning, or gardening. Try to put effort into the chores and think about swapping electrical appliances for "elbow grease"—for example, by using a broom instead of a vacuum cleaner or washing the car by hand instead of going to the car wash.

* When you need to go out to get a newspaper or milk or so on, use the car only if you really need to. Think about walking or even cycling to the stores. Carrying shopping home is a great way to get fitter, burn calories, and improve muscle strength.

* If you commute, consider getting off the bus or train a stop early and walking the rest of the way, or park the car farther away from your workplace. During the working day, stand up whenever you can, walk over to your colleagues' desks to speak to them instead of telephoning or emailing, and use the stairs instead of the escalator or elevator. Don't work through your lunch break at your desk, either; get outside for some fresh air.

Eggs Benedict with Asparagus and Prosciutto

If you are a fan of bacon and eggs, try this—it is rich in protein and fat, which will keep hunger pangs at bay until lunchtime.

Calories 342 // Carbohydrates 15.0 g // Sugars 3.3 g // Protein 20.6 g // Fiber 2.8 g // Fat 25.0 g // Saturated fat 6.0 g // Sodium 960 mg

When you buy eggs, remember that eggs from hens that are allowed to forage and roam freely have a considerably higher Omega-3 fat content than most eggs from caged hens.

8 asparagus spears
4 extra-large eggs
cooking spray, for oiling
8 slices prosciutto
½ cup light mayonnaise
1 tablespoon butter, melted
1 heaping teaspoon dijon mustard
1 tablespoon lemon juice
2 whole-wheat English muffins
pepper, to taste
pinch of cayenne pepper, to garnish

1. Steam the asparagus spears for 5 minutes, or until just tender. Drain and set aside.

2. Meanwhile, poach the eggs in a saucepan of barely simmering water until the whites are set and the yolks are still runny. Transfer to paper towels to drain, set aside, and keep warm.

3. Spray a skillet with cooking spray to coat, then add the prosciutto and cook for 1 minute, or until golden and slightly crisp.

4. Put the mayonnaise, melted butter, mustard, and lemon juice into a bowl, season with pepper, and beat together.

5. Meanwhile, halve and lightly toast the English muffins.

6. Spread each toasted muffin half with a little of the mayonnaise sauce and top with two slices of the prosciutto, two asparagus spears, and a poached egg. Pour the remaining sauce over the top and garnish with a sprinkling of cayenne pepper. Serve immediately.

Serves: 4 // Preparation time: 10–15 minutes // Cooking time: 15 mins

1

2

4

Poached Eggs in Tomato Sauce

Simple and unbelievably delicious, this rustic dish of eggs lightly poached in simmering tomato sauce is perfect for breakfast or brunch.

Calories 312 // Carbohydrates 31.0 g // Sugars 6.4 g // Protein 14.3 g // Fiber 4.5 g // Fat 13.0 g // Saturated fat 3.5 g // Sodium 920 mg

1 tablespoon olive oil
1 small onion, diced
2 garlic cloves, finely chopped
½ teaspoon salt
½ teaspoon pepper
¼ teaspoon crushed red pepper flakes
¼ cup red wine
1 (14½-ounce) can diced tomatoes
2 teaspoons finely chopped fresh oregano, thyme, basil, sage, or other herb
4 eggs
4 thick slices whole-wheat country-style bread (about 1½ ounces each)
2 tablespoons finely chopped Kalamata olives
¼ cup freshly grated Parmesan cheese

1. Heat the oil in a large skillet over medium-high heat. Add the onion and garlic and sauté, stirring occasionally, for about 5 minutes, or until soft. Add the salt, pepper, crushed red pepper flakes, and wine and cook for an additional few minutes, until the liquid has mostly evaporated.

2. Add the tomatoes and their juice, bring to a boil, then reduce the heat to medium-low and simmer for 15–20 minutes, or until the sauce thickens. Stir in the herbs.

3. Make four wells in the sauce and carefully crack an egg into each of them. Cover and simmer for 7–9 minutes, or until the whites are set but the yolks are still runny.

4. Meanwhile, preheat the broiler to medium and lightly toast the bread.

5. Put the slices of toast on four plates. Carefully scoop the eggs out of the sauce and place one on each slice of toast. Place spoonfuls of the sauce around the egg and top with a sprinkling of chopped olives and grated Parmesan cheese. Serve immediately.

Serves: 4 // Preparation time: 10–15 minutes // Cooking time: 35–40 minutes

Tomatoes are rich in potassium, which helps to control high blood pressure, and contain a great range of carotenes as well as vitamins C and E. Research shows that cooking tomatoes in a little oil helps our bodies to absorb these health-giving nutrients more easily.

Spinach Scramble with Toasted Rye Bread

The addition of spinach and rye bread in this recipe turns scrambled eggs into something extra healthy, not to mention extra delicious.

Calories 247 / / Carbohydrates 18.0 g / / Sugars 2.1 g / / Protein 15.3 g / / Fiber 2.8 g / / Fat 12.4 g / / Saturated fat 4.8 g / / Sodium 880 mg

Delicious whole-grain rye bread is believed to improve blood sugar control and regulate appetite. Spinach is rich in vitamin K for bone health, and also in vitamin C, which helps the good amounts of iron in both the eggs and spinach to be absorbed.

1 (6-ounce) package baby spinach, coarsely shredded (about 3 cups)
8 eggs
3 tablespoons skim milk
1 tablespoon butter
4 slices rye bread (about 1 ounce each)
salt and pepper, to taste
freshly grated nutmeg, to serve

1. Heat a large skillet over high heat and add the spinach. Stir for 1–2 minutes, or until the leaves are wilted. Remove from the heat, transfer to a strainer or colander, and squeeze out as much of the excess moisture as possible. Set aside and keep warm.

2. Break the eggs into a bowl, add the milk, and season with salt and pepper. Beat lightly with a fork until evenly mixed.

3. Melt the butter in the pan over medium heat. Add the eggs and stir until just beginning to set. Add the spinach and stir until lightly set.

4. Meanwhile, preheat the broiler to medium and lightly toast the rye bread.

5. Spoon the spinach scramble over the toast, sprinkle with grated nutmeg, and serve immediately.

Serves: 4 / / Preparation time: 10 minutes / / Cooking time: 8–10 minutes

1
2
3

1
2
3

Turkey Sausage Patties with Mushrooms and Tomatoes

These high-protein patties make a wonderful change from regular sausages at breakfast time—they are also great for dinner served with new potatoes.

Calories 239 // Carbohydrates 13.8 g // Sugars 5.0 g // Protein 26.0 g // Fiber 2.7 g // Fat 9.4 g // Saturated fat 2.2 g // Sodium 680 mg

14 ounces ground turkey
1 teaspoon salt
1 teaspoon pepper
1 teaspoon dried thyme
1 teaspoon dried sage
½ teaspoon ground allspice
3 garlic cloves, crushed
¼ cup rolled oats
1 medium egg, beaten
1 tablespoon light olive oil
6½ cups sliced cremini mushrooms
4 tomatoes, cut into wedges

1. Thoroughly combine the turkey with the salt, pepper, thyme, sage, allspice, garlic, oats, and egg in a bowl. (The mixture can be stored, covered, in the refrigerator for up to 12 hours.)

2. Shape the mixture into eight small patties. Heat 2 teaspoons of the oil in a nonstick skillet, add the patties, and cook over medium heat for about 4 minutes on each side, or until golden and cooked all the way through with no pink inside. Transfer to a plate and keep warm.

3. Add the mushrooms to the pan and stir for 1 minute, until soft. Pour in the remaining oil, then add the tomatoes and cook, without stirring, for an additional 1–2 minutes to warm through. Serve the patties with the mushrooms and tomatoes.

Serves: 4 // Preparation time: 15–20 minutes // Cooking time: 15 minutes

If you have a food processor or electric chopper, you can buy turkey leg meat and grind it yourself—the dark leg meat of the turkey contains more B vitamins, selenium, iron, and zinc than the light breast meat.

Potato Pancakes with Smoked Salmon

These crispy potato pancakes topped with dollops of sour cream and slices of smoked salmon are just the thing for a lazy brunch.

Calories 353 / / Carbohydrates 38.0 g / / Sugars 4.4 g / / Protein 18.3 g / / Fiber 4.8 g / / Fat 14.3 g / / Saturated fat 3.6 g / / Sodium 1,000 mg

5 russet or Yukon Gold potatoes (about 1 pound 5 ounces), shredded
1 large onion, grated
2 eggs, lightly beaten
½ cup stale whole-wheat bread crumbs
1 teaspoon salt
pepper, to taste
2 tablespoons sunflower oil
½ cup reduced-fat sour cream
7 ounces thinly sliced smoked salmon
snipped fresh chives, to garnish

1. Preheat the oven to 225°F (or its lowest setting). Line a heatproof plate with paper towels.

2. Working in small batches, put the shredded potatoes onto a dish towel, fold over the dish towel, and squeeze to extract as much water as possible.

3. Put the potatoes into a large bowl and add the onion, eggs, bread crumbs, salt, and pepper to taste. Mix together well.

4. Heat a large, heavy skillet over medium-high heat. Add half the oil and heat until hot. Drop 2 tablespoons of the batter into the skillet and flatten slightly. Add as many more pancakes as will fit in the pan without overcrowding them. Cook for 2 minutes, or until crisp and golden underneath. Flip or turn with a spatula and continue cooking for an additional 1–2 minutes, until crisp and golden.

5. Repeat using the remaining mixture and oil. Meanwhile, transfer the cooked pancakes to the prepared plate and keep warm in the oven.

6. Serve the pancakes hot, topped with the sour cream and smoked salmon. Garnish with chives.

Serves: 4 / / Preparation time: 15–20 minutes / / Cooking time: 8–10 minutes

Surprisingly, shredding the potatoes, as in this recipe, instead of mashing them, helps slow down the rate at which they are absorbed into the digestive system and thus helps minimize the risk of causing a spike in blood sugars.

Lunches

Chicken Noodle Soup

Chicken noodle soup is the perfect comfort food. It is low in fat and saturates and a good source of protein and fiber.

Calories 336 / / Carbohydrates 35.9 g / / Sugars 5.0 g / / Protein 30.6 g / / Fiber 5.3 g / / Fat 7.7 g / / Saturated fat 1.7 g / / Sodium 680 mg

1 tablespoon peanut oil
1 onion, finely chopped
2 celery stalks, finely chopped
1 large carrot, finely chopped
2 garlic cloves, crushed
14 ounces skinless, boneless chicken breasts, cut into bite-size pieces
1½ cup green beans (cut into 1¼-inch-long pieces)
5 cups reduced-sodium chicken broth
pepper, to taste
5½ ounces dried whole-wheat egg noodles
small bunch of fresh cilantro leaves, to garnish

1. Heat the oil in a saucepan over medium heat. Add the onion, celery, and carrot and cook, stirring occasionally, for 8 minutes, until soft but not brown.

2. Add the garlic and cook for 1 minute. Add the chicken to the pan with the beans, broth, and pepper. Bring to a boil, then reduce the heat and simmer for 5 minutes.

3. Add the noodles to the pan, return to a simmer, and cook for 5 minutes, or until the noodles are just tender. Garnish the soup with cilantro leaves and serve immediately.

Serves: 4 / / Preparation time: 15 minutes / / Cooking time: 25 minutes

Peanut oil is excellent to use for frying, because it contains a great balance of healthy monounsaturated and polyunsaturated fats. It also has a mild flavor and a high smoke point, unlike, for example, virgin olive oil.

1
2
3

Split Pea and Ham Soup

Many soups are low in protein, but not this one—it is packed with protein-rich split peas. It needs to be cooked slowly to develop the flavors.

Calories 315 // Carbohydrates 47.1 g // Sugars 8.1 g // Protein 24.1 g // Fiber 18.7 g // Fat 4.4 g // Saturated fat 1.1 g // Sodium 760 mg

- 2½ cups split peas
- 1 tablespoon olive oil
- 1 large onion, finely chopped
- 1 large carrot, finely chopped
- 1 celery stalk, finely chopped
- 3¾ cups reduced-sodium vegetable broth
- 4 cups water
- 8 ounces lean smoked ham, finely diced
- ¼ teaspoon dried thyme
- ¼ teaspoon dried marjoram
- 1 bay leaf
- salt and pepper, to taste

1. Rinse the split peas under cold running water. Put them into a saucepan and cover with water. Bring to a boil and boil for 3 minutes, skimming off any foam from the surface, if necessary. Drain the peas.

2. Heat the oil in a large saucepan over medium heat. Add the onion and sauté for 3–4 minutes, stirring occasionally, until just softened. Add the carrot and celery and continue cooking for 2 minutes.

3. Add the peas, pour the broth and water into the pan, and stir to combine.

4. Bring just to a boil and stir the ham into the soup. Add the thyme, marjoram, and bay leaf. Reduce the heat, cover, and cook gently for 1–1½ hours, until the ingredients are soft. Remove the bay leaf.

5. Taste and adjust the seasoning. Ladle into warm soup bowls and serve.

Serves: 8 // Preparation time: 15 minutes // Cooking time: 1¼ hours–1¾ hours

Split peas are easily digested legumes that are high in resistant starch to maintain stable blood sugar levels. They are a great source of heart-friendly soluble fiber, too, which helps to lower LDL (bad) cholesterol.

1
2
4

Spicy Chickpea and Red Pepper Soup

Chickpeas have been shown to help regulate blood sugar and improve satiety after a meal, making them a useful ingredient in this tasty soup.

Calories 366 // Carbohydrates 44.8 g // Sugars 10.0 g // Protein 13.3 g // Fiber 10.4 g // Fat 14.6 g // Saturated fat 2.7 g // Sodium 240 mg

2½ tablespoons olive oil
6 scallions, chopped
1 large fresh red jalapeño chili, seeded and finely sliced
4 garlic cloves, finely chopped
2 teaspoons ground cumin
1 teaspoon chili powder
3 fresh ripe tomatoes, peeled and coarsely chopped
1 (14-ounce) jar roasted red peppers in water, drained and thinly sliced
1 tablespoon red pepper pesto
3¾ cups reduced-sodium vegetable broth
1 (15-ounce) can chickpeas, drained and rinsed
1 teaspoon granulated stevia
2 teaspoons red wine vinegar
3½ cups baby spinach
pepper, to taste
4 slices oat bread (about 1½ ounces each), to serve

1. Heat the oil in a large saucepan over medium heat. Add the scallions and cook for 2–3 minutes, stirring occasionally, until soft.

2. Add the chili, garlic, cumin, and chili powder and cook for 1 minute, stirring.

3. Stir in the tomatoes, roasted red peppers, pesto, and broth and bring to a simmer. Cook for 10 minutes, then add the chickpeas, stevia, and vinegar, season with pepper, and cook for an additional 5 minutes.

4. Stir in the spinach and cook for 1 minute, until the spinach wilts. Serve with the oat bread.

Serves: 4 // Preparation time: 15 minutes // Cooking time: 25 minutes

For a thicker soup, put half of the soup into a blender at the end of step 3 (before adding the spinach) and blend. Return to the pan with the rest of the soup and stir well.

Mixed Seafood Chowder

Although the East Coast's favorite main-dish soup is normally made with clams, this mixed seafood version is equally as good.

Calories 362 / / Carbohydrates 22.7 g / / Sugars 6.7 g / / Protein 30.4 g / / Fiber 2.3 g / / Fat 15.5 g / / Saturated fat 5.0 g / / Sodium 1,080 mg

1 tablespoon vegetable oil
1 large onion, chopped
2¾ ounces pancetta, cubed
1 tablespoon all-purpose flour
2½ cups fish broth, made from 1 fish bouillon cube
8 ounces small new potatoes, halved
pinch of saffron threads
pinch of cayenne pepper
1¼ cups low-fat milk
7 ounces cod, halibut, or other white fish fillet, cubed
5½ ounces salmon fillet, cubed
7 ounces cooked shelled mussels
black pepper, to taste

1. Heat the oil in a large saucepan over medium heat, then add the onion and pancetta. Cook for 8–10 minutes, until the onion is soft and the pancetta is cooked. Stir in the flour and cook for an additional 2 minutes.

2. Stir in the broth and bring to a gentle simmer. Add the potatoes, then cover and simmer for 10–12 minutes, until the potatoes are tender and cooked through.

3. Add the saffron and cayenne pepper, season with black pepper, then stir in the milk. Add the fish to the pan and simmer gently for 4 minutes.

4. Add the mussels and cook for an additional 2 minutes to warm through. Serve immediately.

Serves: 4 / / Preparation time: 10 minutes / / Cooking time: 30–35 minutes

Both the pancetta and fish broth are high in sodium, so you won't need to add salt to the chowder. If you don't have any saffron threads, you can use ½ teaspoon of sweet paprika instead.

1
2
4

Mini Pizza Muffins

It's great to think that you can have a hearty lunch containing bread, cheese, and crispy ham, knowing its nutrient content is just fine.

Calories 367 / / Carbohydrates 38.6 g / / Sugars 10.3 g / / Protein 25.8 g / / Fiber 7.1 g / / Fat 11.7 g / / Saturated fat 5.3 g / / Sodium 920 mg

These pizza muffins are high in fiber because there are plenty of veggies in each portion, and the whole-wheat flour in the muffins adds more. Whole-wheat English muffins are readily available in supermarkets.

2 whole-wheat English muffins
½ cup prepared tomato sauce with mushrooms
1 tomato, sliced
1¼ cups sliced cremini mushrooms
1 roasted green or yellow pepper from a jar, drained and sliced (3½ ounces drained weight)
2 slices prosciutto, each torn in half
4½ ounces reduced-fat mozzarella cheese, sliced
8 black ripe olives, pitted and sliced

1. Preheat the oven to 350°F. Halve the English muffins and arrange the halves, cut side up, on a baking sheet.

2. Spread a thin layer of tomato sauce on the muffin halves, then top with the sliced tomato and mushrooms.

3. Divide the roasted pepper among the muffin halves, then top with the prosciutto, mozzarella cheese, and olives.

4. Bake in the preheated oven for 15 minutes, or until the cheese is melted and the English muffins are toasted. Serve immediately.

Serves: 2 / / Preparation time: 10 minutes / / Cooking time: 15 minutes

1
2
3

1
3
4

Pulled Pork Wraps

Slow-cooked pulled pork is deservedly popular and these wraps won't disappoint. The leftover pork can be frozen for another time.

Calories 467 // Carbohydrates 43.8 g // Sugars 10.1 g // Protein 24.3 g // Fiber 3.9 g // Fat 17.1 g // Saturated fat 1.2 g // Sodium 920 mg

1 small pork shoulder (about 2¼ pounds), skin removed
1 teaspoon salt
2 teaspoons sweet paprika
2 teaspoons packed light brown sugar
1 teaspoon dijon mustard
½ cup reduced-sodium chicken broth

To Serve

8 crisp lettuce leaves
6 scallions, chopped
¼ cucumber, chopped
½ cup fresh cilantro leaves
1 mild red chili, sliced
3 tablespoons chili dipping sauce
juice of ½ lime
4 multigrain tortillas

1. Preheat the oven to 425°F. Line a roasting pan with a piece of aluminum foil large enough to cover the pork. Put the pork into the pan, rub ½ teaspoon of the salt and 1 teaspoon of the paprika into the skin, and cook in the preheated oven (without covering) for 30 minutes.

2. Reduce the oven temperature to 300°F. Rub the remaining salt and paprika into the pork along with the sugar and mustard. Pour in the broth and loosely cover with the foil. Cook for an additional 3 hours, or until the pork is soft and a piece comes away from the roast easily when pulled with a fork.

3. Increase the oven temperature to 425°F and cook the pork for an additional 20 minutes, until crisp on the outside. Remove from the oven and let rest, covered, for 30 minutes.

4. Pull the pork into pieces with two forks. Pour any cooking juices over the pulled pork and stir to combine. Measure out 3 cups of the pork and use this to make the wraps.

5. Divide the pork, lettuce, scallions, cucumber, cilantro, chili, chili sauce, and lime juice among the wraps. Serve immediately.

Serves: 4 // Preparation time: 20 minutes // Cooking time: 3 hours 50 minutes, plus resting

You can use the leftover pulled pork cold to fill a whole-wheat sandwich or pita bread, along with plenty of salad.

Chicken and Corn Burritos

Burritos are fun to make and you can vary the ingredients—try black beans instead of pinto beans and use turkey instead of chicken.

Calories 361 // Carbohydrates 39.2 g // Sugars 4.6 g // Protein 22.1 g // Fiber 6.2 g // Fat 12.6 g // Saturated fat 4.1 g // Sodium 520 mg

These tasty lunch snacks have an almost perfect nutritional profile—they are low in fat and saturates, and packed with protein, fiber, and resistant starch to keep your blood sugar on an even keel.

1 tablespoon olive oil
8 ounces skinless, boneless chicken breasts, cut into strips
¾ cup corn kernels
⅔ cup canned pinto beans, drained and rinsed
⅔ cup cooked quinoa
2 teaspoons hot chili sauce
juice of 1 lime
½ cup light cream cheese with garlic and herbs
1½ cups thinly shredded green cabbage
4 whole-wheat tortillas
½ cup fresh cilantro leaves
pepper, to taste

1. Heat the oil in a nonstick skillet over high heat. Add the chicken to the pan and stir for 1–2 minutes, or until browned. Stir in the corn and beans and cook until the corn is slightly browned.

2. Add the quinoa, chili sauce, lime juice, cream cheese, and cabbage. Season with pepper. Cook, stirring, over medium-high heat for a few minutes, until the cheese has melted.

3. Divide the mixture among the tortillas, sprinkle with the cilantro, and roll up. Serve immediately.

Serves: 4 // Preparation time: 10 minutes // Cooking time: 8–10 minutes

1
2
3

Top Ten Superfoods for Diabetes

1. Legumes

Legumes, such as chickpeas, lentils, and kidney beans, are high in soluble and insoluble fibers and resistant starch; have a good carbohydrate to protein ratio; boast a low GI rating of around 30; and contain essential vitamins and minerals—making them an all-round superfood for diabetics. Research shows that regularly eating legumes can reduce the risk of heart disease, control blood sugar levels, and lower blood pressure.

2. Oily fish

Oily fish, such as salmon, mackerel, and fresh tuna, are great sources of Omega-3 fats, which lower the risk of heart disease by improving the blood fats profile, slowing the growth rate of arterial plaques, and lowering blood pressure. The fat is also anti-inflammatory, and oily fish has a great content of vitamin D, deficiency of which may be linked to type 2 diabetes.

3. Nuts

There is evidence that nuts can improve blood sugar control in type 2 diabetics and can also reduce LDL (low density lipoproteins or "bad") cholesterol and even help with weight loss. Nuts are low on the glycemic index and contain important nutrients, including monounsaturated and polyunsaturated fats, magnesium, and vitamin E.

4. Seeds

Flaxseed, pine nuts, sunflower seeds, and pumpkin seeds are particularly good sources of essential fats and monounsaturated fats. Flaxseed are high in the Omega-3 fat ALA (alpha linolenic acid), linked with protection from heart disease, stroke, and inflammation. Diets supplemented with flaxseed result in lowered fasting blood glucose levels and reduced blood pressure, total cholesterol, and LDL cholesterol.

5. Oats

Oats are full of soluble and insoluble fiber, which help to metabolize fats, keep the digestive tract healthy, and keep blood sugar stable by delaying the speed at which the stomach empties. Compared to other grains, oats have a higher proportion of soluble fiber, which can help to lower LDL cholesterol and decrease the risk of heart disease.

6. Berries

Berries have among the lowest GI ratings of all fruit types and can help with blood sugar control. They are also high in plant compounds called anthocyanins—a large study published in the *American Journal of Clinical Nutrition* has found that people who regularly consume berries have up to 23 percent lower risk of developing type 2 diabetes than those who don't. In addition, raspberries contain ellagic acid, which can reduce insulin resistance, lower blood sugars, and counter inflammation.

7. Leafy greens

Greens, such as cabbage, spinach, Swiss chard, and broccoli, contain plenty of antioxidant compounds (such as lutein and zeaxanthin to help keep eyes healthy), vitamins, and calcium to help maintain bone density. Greens can help to lower high blood pressure, and sulforaphane—a plant compound in broccoli—may help to prevent damage caused to the blood vessels by diabetes.

8. Yogurt

Yogurt and other dairy foods, such as skim milk and hard cheese, can promote good bone health, reduce blood pressure, and help the body burn more fat. It is thought that the calcium they contain may bind with fat and prevent its absorption. Yogurt with live or "probiotic" cultures can also support immune health and protect against developing type 2 diabetes.

9. Avocados

Avocados are known for their heart-healthy oleic acid (a type of monounsaturated fat) content, which can improve cholesterol and blood lipids profile, decrease the risk of cardiovascular disease, and may also reduce the risk of developing type 2 diabetes. The fruits are also rich in potassium, which can help to reduce blood pressure.

10. Tomatoes

Tomatoes, unlike many fruits, have a moderate GI rating of 55 or less and also a low GL because of their low calorie content. Dietitians recommend fresh tomatoes as a fruit that diabetics can eat to satisfy appetite. Regular consumption helps to reduce high blood pressure, and research shows it may also help to reduce the risk of cardiovascular disease associated with type 2 diabetes.

Crustless Zucchini and Fava Bean Quiche

This reduced-fat, reduced-calorie quiche has a thin, whole-wheat pastry shell but no crust around the edges, making a perfect summer lunch.

Calories 412 / / Carbohydrates 37.7 g / / Sugars 4.7 g / / Protein 16.8 g / / Fiber 7.1 g / / Fat 19.0 g / / Saturated fat 7.0 g / / Sodium 1,000 mg

1. Lightly rub together the flour and margarine in a mixing bowl until it resembles fine bread crumbs. Add the salt and stir, then stir in the water and mix until a ball forms. Wrap the dough in plastic wrap and let chill in the refrigerator for 30 minutes.

2. Meanwhile, preheat the broiler to high. Put the zucchini sticks onto a baking sheet and spray with cooking spray to coat, then cook under the preheated broiler until slightly charred and soft, turning halfway through. Steam the fava beans until just tender. Add the eggs, milk, cheese, mint, and nutmeg to a bowl, season with salt and pepper, and combine.

3. Preheat the oven to 375°F. Remove the dough from the refrigerator and roll out on a lightly floured surface into a rough circle, then cut out a neat circle using an 8-inch tart dish as a guide.

4. Line the bottom of the dish with the pastry circle and prick all over. Cover with parchment paper and pie weights or dried beans and bake in the preheated oven for 15 minutes. Remove the paper and weights and return to the oven for an additional 5 minutes.

5. Spray the inside edges of the tart dish with cooking spray. Spoon the zucchini, fava beans, and potatoes evenly into the dish, then gently pour in the egg mixture. Return to the oven and bake for 25 minutes, or until the filling is set but still with some wobble, and the top is golden.

6. Let cool in the dish for 15 minutes. Serve warm or cold with the salad greens.

Serves: 4 / / Preparation time: 25 minutes, plus chilling / / Cooking time: 1 hour, plus cooling

1¼ cups spelt flour, plus extra for dusting
5 tablespoons margarine (from a block), chopped
½ teaspoon salt
2 tablespoons water
9 ounces zucchini, cut into ¼-inch-thick sticks
cooking spray, for oiling
⅔ cup fava beans
3 eggs
1 cup low-fat milk
¼ cup freshly grated Parmesan cheese
2 tablespoons chopped fresh mint
pinch of freshly grated nutmeg
4½ ounces baby new potatoes, unpeeled, cut into ½-inch dice
salt and pepper, to taste
7 cups mixed salad greens, to serve

Try to find baby fava beans so that you can enjoy eating them (once you've removed them from their pods) without having to remove the outer pale green skins, which contain much of the fiber in these low-GI vegetables.

1
2
5

Avocado, Artichoke, and Almond Salad

This beautiful salad is full of healthy ingredients, giving you plenty of heart-friendly monounsaturated fats and a huge boost of fiber.

Calories 364 // Carbohydrates 31.0 g // Sugars 4.1 g // Protein 9.0 g // Fiber 13.4 g // Fat 24.0 g // Saturated fat 3.0 g // Sodium 560 mg

1 red mini romaine lettuce, tough outer leaves discarded
6 artichoke hearts in water from a can or jar, drained and patted dry
1 small yellow bell pepper, seeded and thinly sliced
2 ripe avocados, peeled, pitted, and sliced
1¾ cups mâche or other peppery salad greens
⅓ cup slivered almonds
4 radishes, finely chopped
8 dark rye crispbreads, to serve

Dressing
3 tablespoons balsamic vinegar
1 tablespoon olive oil
½ teaspoon salt
pepper, to taste

1. Cut about ½ inch from the bottom of the romaine lettuce. Peel off the outer leaves and reserve. Cut the heart lengthwise into eight pieces and arrange on a serving plate with the reserved leaves.

2. Halve the artichoke hearts and add to the serving plate with the yellow bell pepper and avocados.

3. Sprinkle with the mâche or other greens, slivered almonds, and radishes.

4. For the dressing, put the vinegar, oil, and salt into a small bowl, season with pepper, and whisk thoroughly, then drizzle it over the salad. Serve immediately with the crispbreads.

Serves: 4 // Preparation time: 15 minutes // Cooking time: None

You can use artichoke hearts that have been canned in oil or water, but avoid those stored in salted water. Look for mâche or other peppery greens at a farmer's market and choose whatever looks best.

Eggplant Paprika Salad

This warm salad is a great way to eat eggplants, bringing you smoky flavors, a variety of textures, and warm spices all on one plate.

Calories 475 / / Carbohydrates 56.3 g / / Sugars 10.6 g / / Protein 12.9 g / / Fiber 14.1 g / / Fat 19.8 g / / Saturated fat 2.5 g / / Sodium 680 mg

2 eggplants
2 tablespoons olive oil
2 red bell peppers, seeded and cut into 6 pieces each
1 (15-ounce) can chickpeas, drained and rinsed
1 red onion, finely chopped
4 whole-wheat pita breads, to serve

Dressing
3 tablespoons olive oil
juice of ½ lemon
1 teaspoon ground coriander
1 teaspoon ground cumin
2 teaspoons smoked paprika
1 teaspoon granulated stevia
small bunch of fresh cilantro, leaves removed and reserved and stems chopped
salt and pepper, to taste

1. Preheat the broiler to high. Cut the eggplants lengthwise into ½ inch-thick slices, brush with oil on both sides, and arrange on a broiler rack. Add the red bell pepper pieces. Cook under the preheated broiler until the eggplants are charred in patches on the top side; turn over and cook until the eggplants are soft and the red bell pepper pieces are lightly cooked and slightly brown in places. Remove from the heat but do not turn off the broiler.

2. Cut the eggplant slices into large bite-size pieces and put into a shallow serving dish with the red bell pepper pieces, chickpeas, and red onion.

3. To make the dressing, combine the oil, lemon juice, ground coriander, ground cumin, paprika, and stevia with salt and pepper in a small bowl. Add the cilantro stems to the dressing and stir to combine. Spoon the dressing evenly over the salad and stir—it's best to do this while the vegetables are still warm.

4. Meanwhile, toast the pita breads under the broiler.

5. Sprinkle the salad with the reserved cilantro leaves and serve with the pita breads.

Serves: 4 / / Preparation time: 15 minutes / / Cooking time: 20 minutes

Research shows that a diet high in legumes, such as chickpeas, may reduce markers for blood sugar in people with type 2 diabetes even more successfully than a whole-grain diet.

1
3
3

1
2
3

Rib Eye Steak Salad with Arugula and Parmesan

This warm salad is extremely quick to make yet bursting with flavors. Rib eye is one of the tastiest steak cuts you can find.

Calories 413 / / Carbohydrates 20.4 g / / Sugars 4.4 g / / Protein 36.0 g / / Fiber 3.4 g / / Fat 17.4 g / / Saturated fat 5.3 g / / Sodium 480 mg

4 rib eye steaks (about 5½ oz each), trimmed
2½ cups arugula
2½ cups watercress or other peppery salad greens
4 tomatoes, cut into wedges
1½ ounces Parmesan cheese shavings, to garnish
4 slices seeded, whole-wheat bread (about 1½ ounces each), to serve

Dressing
3 tablespoons balsamic vinegar
juice of ½ lemon
2 tablespoons olive oil
1 large garlic clove, crushed
½ teaspoon salt
pepper, to taste

1. Heat a ridged grill pan until hot, then add the steaks and cook for 2 minutes. Turn and cook for an additional minute for rare to medium-rare. (For medium, cook for 3 minutes, turn, and cook for another 1½ minutes; for well done, cook for 3½ minutes, turn, and cook for another 2 minutes.)

2. Transfer the cooked steaks to a plate, cover, and let rest for 5–6 minutes. Meanwhile, arrange the arugula, watercress, and tomato wedges on serving plates.

3. To make the dressing, combine the vinegar, lemon juice, oil, garlic, salt, and pepper in a bowl.

4. Pour the meat juices that have collected on the cooked steak plate into the dressing. Cut each steak into ½ inch-thick slices and arrange on the serving plates. Add any juices from the board to the dressing and drizzle the dressing over the salads.

5. Arrange the Parmesan cheese shavings on top of the salads. Serve immediately with the bread.

Serves: 4 / / Preparation time: 10 minutes / / Cooking time: 5–8 minutes, plus resting

Beef is packed with protein to help to stave off hunger. It is also a great source of easily absorbed iron, which is useful because diabetics are more prone to anemia, and of the B vitamins, which can be deficient in diabetics.

Smoked Mackerel, Beet, and New Potato Salad

One of the best flavor pairings you will find is smoked mackerel and beets, and this unusual salad is a great way to use this combination.

Calories 435 // Carbohydrates 26.0 g // Sugars 10.0 g // Protein 24.6 g // Fiber 5.8 g // Fat 26.9 g // Saturated fat 5.2 g // Sodium 880 mg

- 6 raw beets (about 1 pound 2 ounces), peeled and quartered
- 2½ tablespoons olive oil
- 2 tablespoons balsamic vinegar
- 10½ ounces baby new potatoes, unpeeled
- cooking spray, for coating
- 2½ cups arugula
- 13 ounces smoked mackerel fillets
- 8 red radishes, thinly sliced
- pepper, to taste

1. Preheat the oven to 350°F. Line a roasting pan with aluminum foil. Put the beets into a bowl.

2. In a small bowl, thoroughly combine the oil and vinegar and spoon a little under half of it into the bowl with the beets. Stir well to coat the beets, then arrange them on one side of the prepared roasting pan. Transfer any dressing remaining in the beet bowl back into the small bowl. Bake the beets in the preheated oven for 25 minutes.

3. Meanwhile, cook the new potatoes in a saucepan of simmering water until just tender, then arrange on the other side of the roasting pan and spray them with cooking spray to coat. Turn the beets and cook for an additional 20 minutes, or until the beets are cooked through and the outsides of the potatoes are slightly crisp. Let cool until just warm.

4. Meanwhile, arrange the arugula on a serving dish and flake the mackerel. Arrange the beets and potatoes on the serving dish with the mackerel and sprinkle with the sliced radishes. Combine any juices remaining in the roasting pan with the remaining dressing and drizzle it over the salad. Add a grinding of pepper and serve while the beets and potatoes are still just warm.

Serves: 4 // Preparation time: 10 minutes // Cooking time: 45 minutes, plus cooling

Many people who have diabetes also have high blood pressure, and beets have been proven, when eaten regularly, to lower blood pressure convincingly, while mackerel is rich in heart-friendly Omega-3 fats.

2
3
3

Lentil and Tuna Salad

This recipe combines tuna, lentils, tomatoes, and red onion for a protein-packed lunch that will help you stay focused all afternoon.

Calories 225 / / Carbohydrates 15.7 g / / Sugars 3.2 g / / Protein 16.2 g / / Fiber 5.9 g / / Fat 14.1 g / / Saturated fat 1.9 g / / Sodium 200 mg

2 ripe tomatoes
1 small red onion
2 cups cooked brown or green lentils
1 (5-ounce) can chunk light tuna in water, drained
2 tablespoons chopped fresh cilantro
pepper, to taste

Dressing
3 tablespoons virgin olive oil
1 tablespoon lemon juice
1 teaspoon whole-grain mustard
1 garlic clove, crushed
½ teaspoon ground cumin
½ teaspoon ground coriander

1. Using a sharp knife, seed the tomatoes and dice them. Finely chop the red onion.

2. To make the dressing, beat all the dressing ingredients into a small bowl until thoroughly combined. Set aside until required.

3. Mix together the chopped onion, diced tomatoes, and cooked lentils in a large bowl.

4. Flake the tuna with a fork and stir it into the lentil mixture. Stir in the chopped cilantro and mix well.

5. Pour the dressing over the salad and season with pepper. Serve immediately.

Serves: 4 / / Preparation time: 15 minutes / / Cooking time: None

Lentils, particularly the black, brown, and green types, are one of the most nutritious foods, and their high levels of soluble and total fiber can help to prevent diverticular disease and other digestive disorders.

Little Curried Crab Cakes with Avocado Salad

Once you've done the preparation, these little crab cakes are easy to put together, and are perfectly complemented by the tangy avocado salad.

Calories 362 // Carbohydrates 40.0 g // Sugars 3.9 g // Protein 23.7 g // Fiber 7.7 g // Fat 14.0 g // Saturated fat 2.3 g // Sodium 520 mg

1. Mix together the crabmeat, corn, bread crumbs, egg, mayonnaise, yogurt, chives, mustard, curry powder, and pepper in a bowl.

2. Using your hands, shape the mixture into eight patties. Spray a nonstick skillet with cooking spray to coat, then heat to just below medium-hot and add the patties to the pan. Cook the patties for 4 minutes, without turning or moving them.

3. Meanwhile, make the salad. Pit, peel, and slice the avocado, then lightly crush it in a bowl. Add the tomato, lime juice, cilantro leaves, chili, and scallions and stir to combine.

4. Spray the tops of the patties with more cooking spray, then use a metal spatula to turn each one over carefully. Cook for an additional 3 minutes, or until the crab cakes are golden and piping hot. Serve immediately with the avocado salad.

Serves: 4 // Preparation time: 20 minutes // Cooking time: 8 minutes

10½ ounces white crabmeat
1 cup canned drained corn kernels
1 cup whole-wheat panko bread crumbs
1 extra-large egg, beaten
1½ tablespoons light mayonnaise
1½ tablespoons fat-free Greek-style yogurt
2 tablespoons snipped fresh chives
2 teaspoons dijon mustard
1 teaspoon curry powder
¼ teaspoon pepper
cooking spray, for oiling

Salad
1 large ripe avocado
1 tomato, finely chopped
juice of ½ lime
small bunch of fresh cilantro, leaves only
½ fresh red jalapeño chile, seeded and finely chopped
3 scallions, chopped

Panko bread crumbs, originating from Japan, are available in most supermarkets, although you may need to look online for the whole-wheat type. Light and flaky, they make all the difference to the texture of these fish cakes.

1
2
3

Dinners

Chili Con Carne

One of the most popular family meals—chili con carne—is transformed into one of the healthiest with just a few sneaky tweaks.

Calories 622 / / Carbohydrates 82.4 g / / Sugars 8.4 g / / Protein 35.3 g / / Fiber 11.3 g / / Fat 16.0 g / / Saturated fat 3.1 g / / Sodium 640 mg

1. Heat the oil in a large nonstick skillet over medium-high heat. Add the beef and cook, stirring occasionally, for a few minutes, until browned all over.

2. Push the beef to the side of the pan, then add the onion, celery, and garlic. Reduce the heat to medium-low, cover, and cook for 5 minutes, until the vegetables are soft but not browned.

3. Stir in the green bell pepper, tomatoes, tomato paste, chili paste, red pepper flakes, ground coriander, ground cumin, ½ teaspoon of the salt, and pepper to taste. Bring to a simmer, reduce the heat to low, then replace the lid, and cook for 25 minutes.

4. Meanwhile, cook the rice with the remaining salt according to the package directions until tender, then drain.

5. Add the mushrooms and kidney beans to the beef mixture and stir. Bring back to a simmer and cook for an additional 5 minutes. Garnish the chili with the parsley and serve immediately with the rice.

Serves: 4 / / Preparation time: 15–20 minutes / / Cooking time: 45 minutes

- 1 tablespoon canola oil
- 14 ounces ground round or ground sirloin beef
- 1 large onion, finely chopped
- 2 celery stalks, chopped
- 3 garlic cloves, finely chopped
- 1 large green bell pepper, seeded and coarsely chopped
- 1 (14½-ounce) can diced tomatoes
- 1 tablespoon tomato paste
- 2 tablespoons chili paste
- 1–2 teaspoons crushed red pepper flakes
- ½ teaspoon ground coriander
- ½ teaspoon ground cumin
- 1 teaspoon salt
- 1⅔ cups brown long-grain rice (preferably basmati)
- 3 cups sliced white button mushrooms
- 1 (15-ounce) canned red kidney beans, drained and rinsed
- pepper, to taste
- 2 tablespoons chopped fresh flat-leaf parsley, to garnish

The amount of fat in ground beef isn't always labeled; if you can't find one labeled 10 percent fat, choose by the color—the redder the meat, the less amount of fat. A higher fat content will be too high in saturates; any lower, too dry.

1

2

4

Spaghetti and Meatballs

Packed with warming flavors and textures, this is a hearty low-cost meal idea that is perfect for chilly fall or winter evenings.

Calories 585 // Carbohydrates 74.5 g // Sugars 11.7 g // Protein 36.4 g // Fiber 8.0 g // Fat 16.4 g // Saturated fat 4.1 g // Sodium 600 mg

1 cup fresh white bread crumbs
¼ cup skim milk
14 ounces fresh lean ground pork
1 onion, finely chopped
2 garlic cloves, crushed
2 tablespoons chopped fresh parsley
2 teaspoons crushed fennel seeds
1 tablespoon olive oil
10½ ounces dried spelt spaghetti or whole-wheat spaghetti
salt and pepper, to taste
fresh basil leaves, to garnish

Sauce

4½ ounces zucchini, shredded
3 garlic cloves, finely grated
1 (28-ounce) can diced tomatoes
1 tablespoon tomato paste
1 teaspoon maple syrup
1 teaspoon red wine vinegar

1. Mix the bread crumbs with the milk and let soak for a few minutes, then transfer to a mixing bowl, add the pork, onion, garlic, parsley, and fennel seeds, season with salt and pepper, and mix all the ingredients together. Shape into 16 meatballs, transferring each to a plate as you make them.

2. Heat the oil in a large skillet with a lid. Add the meatballs and cook, uncovered, over medium-high heat for a few minutes, turning occasionally, until slightly brown. Transfer to a plate with a slotted spoon, cover, and set aside.

3. To make the sauce, reduce the heat to medium and add the shredded zucchini to the skillet. Cook for 1–2 minutes, then add the garlic and cook for a few seconds.

4. Add the tomatoes, tomato paste, maple syrup, and vinegar, mix thoroughly, and bring to a gentle simmer. Cover and cook for 15 minutes, then remove the lid and cook, stirring occasionally, for an additional 10 minutes.

5. Return the meatballs to the pan and stir to coat in the sauce, then cook for an additional 10 minutes, or until about half the liquid has evaporated and you have a rich sauce.

6. Meanwhile, bring a large saucepan of lightly salted water to a boil. Add the spaghetti and cook for 8–10 minutes, or according to package directions, until tender but still firm to the bite. Drain the spaghetti, transfer to a serving plate, and spoon the tomato sauce and meatballs on top. Garnish with basil leaves and serve immediately.

Serves: 4 // Preparation time: 25–30 minutes // Cooking time: 50 minutes

If you haven't tried spelt spaghetti before, try it now. It is more widely available, has a delicious nutty flavor, and a texture similar to whole-wheat spaghetti.

Chinese Marinated Flank Steak with Noodles

Flank steak is an underused cut of beef that lends itself well to Asian flavors. It can be cooked quickly, just like more expensive cuts of steak.

Calories 533 / / Carbohydrates 60.0 g / / Sugars 4.0g / / Protein 38.8 g / / Fiber 6.0 g / / Fat 16.4 g / / Saturated fat 4.8 g / / Sodium 360 mg

1 pound 2 ounces thick flank steak, fat trimmed
9¾ ounces dried whole-wheat noodles
1 large red bell pepper, seeded and thinly sliced
6 scallions, sliced diagonally
2 teaspoons sesame oil
1½ cups fresh bean sprouts

Marinade

4 teaspoons sesame oil
2 tablespoons rice wine vinegar
4 garlic cloves, crushed
1 tablespoon finely chopped ginger
1 fresh red jalapeño chili, sliced
1 tablespoon teriyaki sauce
1 tablespoon light soy sauce

1. To make the marinade, combine all the ingredients in a small bowl.

2. Put the steak in a nonmetallic shallow bowl just large enough to fit it, pour the marinade over it, then cover with plastic wrap. Let stand at room temperature for at least 1 hour.

3. Preheat a large skillet over high heat. Remove the steak from the marinade (reserving the marinade), add to the pan, and cook for 3 minutes on each side. Remove the pan from the heat, take the steak out of the pan, and cut it into thick strips, slicing against the grain. Set aside on a warm plate to rest and keep warm.

4. Cook or soak the noodles according to the package directions and drain.

5. Add the red bell pepper and scallions to the skillet with the oil and stir-fry over high heat for 2 minutes. Reduce the heat to medium, add the reserved marinade to the pan, and stir for 1 minute, then add the noodles and bean sprouts to the pan and stir for an additional minute.

6. Serve the noodle mixture with the pieces of steak on top, drizzled with any juices from the plate.

Serves: 4 / / Preparation time: 15 minutes, plus marinating / / Cooking time: 20 minutes

Adding plenty of spices, such as chili, garlic, and ginger, to your diet is healthy, because they contain a variety of antioxidant compounds that can help to reduce the risk of heart disease.

1

2

5

1
2
3

Turkey Paprika Tacos

Turkey makes a great change from chicken in almost any dish, and its somewhat richer flavor lends itself well to Mexican-style meals like this.

Calories 321 // Carbohydrates 31.4 g // Sugars 5.3 g // Protein 29.7 g // Fiber 6.7 g // Fat 8.0 g // Saturated fat 4.1 g // Sodium 400 mg

10½ ounces skinless, boneless turkey breasts, cut into strips
2 garlic cloves, crushed
2 teaspoons smoked paprika
juice of ½ lime
1 red onion, chopped
1 tomato, chopped
½ cup cooked black beans
2 cups shredded crisp lettuce
4 whole-wheat tortillas
⅓ cup shredded reduced-fat cheddar cheese or American cheese
2 teaspoons hot pepper sauce
⅓ cup reduced-fat sour cream

1. Put the turkey strips into a nonmetallic shallow bowl. Stir in the garlic with the paprika and lime juice. Cover and let marinate for 30 minutes.

2. Meanwhile, combine the onion, tomato, black beans, and lettuce in a bowl.

3. Preheat the broiler to medium-hot. Line a baking sheet with aluminum foil. Put the turkey strips on the prepared baking sheet and cook under the preheated broiler for about 6 minutes, turning once, until golden brown and cooked through. Set aside.

4. Heat the tortillas under the broiler until slightly golden and crisp. Divide the turkey and the bean mixture evenly among the tortillas, arranging them on only one half of the tortilla. Sprinkle with the cheese and drizzle with the hot pepper sauce and sour cream. Fold the tacos to serve.

Serves: 4 // Preparation time: 15 minutes, plus marinating // Cooking time: 8 minutes

Black beans are a rich source of resistant starch. You can buy dried black beans and soak and cook them yourself, or choose beans that are canned or boxed in water (not salt water).

Chicken Scallops with Cherry Tomatoes

These succulent chicken cutlets make a wonderful light supper and are ideal for days when you have had a higher-carbohydrate lunch.

Calories 342 / / Carbohydrates 28.0 g / / Sugars 3.9 g / / Protein 32.7 g / / Fiber 2.1 g / / Fat 12.0 g / / Saturated fat 2.1 g / / Sodium 280 mg

3 skinless, boneless chicken breasts (about 1 pound 2 ounces)
1 egg, beaten
1 cup whole-wheat panko bread crumbs
1 teaspoon dried thyme
1 teaspoon dried oregano
2 tablespoons peanut oil
24 cherry tomatoes, on the vine
7 cups mixed baby salad greens
1 tablespoon balsamic vinegar

1. Diagonally slice each chicken breast in four lengthwise to make 12 cutlets. Place each cutlet on a cutting board and pound it a few times with a rolling pin to a thickness of about ½ inch.

2. Put the beaten egg into a shallow dish and put the bread crumbs into a separate shallow dish. Add the thyme and oregano to the dish of bread crumbs and stir to combine.

3. Coat each scallop in egg, then hold it above the egg dish to let the excess drip off. Dip into the bread crumb mixture, turning to coat, then transfer to a large plate.

4. Heat the oil in a large, nonstick skillet. Add the chicken, in batches, and cook over medium heat for about 4 minutes on each side, until the bread crumbs are golden brown and the chicken is cooked all the way through.

5. Meanwhile, preheat the broiler and broil the tomatoes on the vine until warmed through but not collapsed.

6. Serve the chicken with the tomatoes and the baby salad greens, drizzled with the vinegar.

Serves: 4 / / Preparation time: 15 minutes / / Cooking time: 25 minutes

Balsamic vinegar is extremely useful as a quick and easy salad dressing. Each tablespoon contains just 14 calories, and it is free from fat and salt. It is worth buying a more expensive aged balsamic for its taste and texture.

1
3 
4

Eating Out

Of course, you want a special meal if you're eating out at a great restaurant or your favorite café, especially if you don't do it often. The good news is that there's usually plenty on any menu that you can eat without having to feel guilty the next day. However, statistics show that food eaten out contains on average at least 50 percent more fat and calories than the meals you eat at home, so it pays to use a few tips to minimize the potential for dietary disaster.

* If you're eating in a restaurant, decide beforehand whether you're going to have an appetizer or a dessert along with your main dish instead of both.

* If possible, check the menu (many restaurants have them available online) before you go to a restaurant and try to decide what you're going to eat. It will often save you from making less wise choices on the spur of the moment.

* If you are having more than one course, try to balance out the courses in the same way that you would balance a meal at home—for example, one high-carbohydrate course balances one high-protein course, or one low-fat course balances one high-fat course.

* Add as many vegetables or as much salad to your plate as you can. If you're having a main dish with a rich sauce, try to accompany it with plainly cooked vegetables.

* Try to avoid "white" carbohydrates (such as white bread, white rice, and white pasta), instead choosing whole-wheat or whole-grain versions.

* Instead of having a side of potatoes, see if the restaurant will serve you lower-GI sweet potatoes; a protein-rich grain (such as quinoa); or mashed legumes (such as a white bean puree), which have a great balance of protein and carbohydrates.

* Try to pick an eating establishment where you aren't kept waiting a long time to begin eating, which may tempt you to fill up on the bread basket and/or drink alcohol to pass the time.

* If you have to watch your weight, it is best to avoid restaurants and cafés that offer help-yourself buffets or "all-you-can-eat" deals. Research shows that people continue to eat at this type of venue even when they are full.

* Some of the dishes that are probably high in calories and fat include pastry dishes; many meat and cream-based dishes at Indian and Thai restaurants; rich pasta dishes, such as lasagna and pasta carbonara, and most pizzas at Italian restaurants; and French dishes, such as hearty cassoulets with pork, lamb, or sausages.

* Some dishes probably lower in calories and fat include lean steak, venison, or chicken; Japanese food; vegetable and seafood stir-fries; broiled, grilled, or baked fish; noncreamy vegetable soups or broths; and meat, poultry, seafood, and vegetable skewers.

1
2
5

Chicken Chow Mein

This popular Chinese dish is simple to make, and once you've prepared your ingredients, it can be on the table in just over 10 minutes.

Calories 469 / / Carbohydrates 65.0 g / / Sugars 9.4 g / / Protein 29.0 g / / Fiber 7.2 g / / Fat 9.6 g / / Saturated fat 1.4 g / / Sodium 800 mg

1. To make the sauce, crush the garlic with the flat edge of the blade of a large knife. Put the garlic and ginger into a small bowl with the ketchup, oyster sauce, soy sauce, broth, and sesame oil. Stir well to combine and set aside.

2. Bring a large saucepan of water to a boil, add the noodles, and cook for 4 minutes, or according to the package directions. Meanwhile, put the chicken into a bowl, add the soy sauce, and toss to coat.

3. Drain the noodles and set aside. Heat half the peanut oil in a wok or large, deep skillet until hot, then stir in the chicken and cook for 2–3 minutes. Remove from the wok and set aside.

4. Add the orange bell pepper, scallions, carrots, broccoli, snow peas, and the remaining peanut oil to the wok and stir for 1–2 minutes, until browned and soft. Add the sauce, stir again, and let simmer for 1–2 minutes.

5. Return the chicken to the wok and add the mushrooms and bean sprouts, stirring for an additional minute. Stir in the noodles to warm through and serve immediately.

Serves: 4 / / Preparation time: 25 minutes / / Cooking time: 15–18 minutes

9 ounces dried whole-wheat noodles
2 skinless, boneless chicken breasts (about 10½ ounces), cut into 1¼-inch strips
1 tablespoon reduced-sodium soy sauce
1 tablespoon peanut oil
1 large orange bell pepper, seeded and thinly sliced
8 scallions, diagonally sliced
2 small carrots (about 3½ ounces), thinly sliced
1½ cups small broccoli florets
1 cup snow peas
3½ ounces Asian mushrooms, such as shiitake, sliced if large
3 cups fresh bean sprouts

Sauce
3 garlic cloves, coarsely chopped
1-inch piece fresh ginger, finely chopped
2 tablespoons reduced-sodium ketchup
1 tablespoon oyster sauce
1 tablespoon reduced-sodium soy sauce
½ cup reduced-sodium chicken broth
1 tablespoon sesame oil

Recent research links Asian mushrooms with protection from cardiovascular disease.

Chicken and Shrimp Jambalaya

The name sounds fun and cheerful, and so is the look and taste of this dish with its riot of colors, flavors, and textures.

Calories 548 / / Carbohydrates 52.0 g / / Sugars 7.0 g / / Protein 44.7 g / / Fiber 5.2 g / / Fat 17.6 g / / Saturated fat 3.8 g / / Sodium 640 mg

1 tablespoon canola oil
4 large skinless, boneless chicken thighs (about 1 pound 2 ounces), each cut into 3 pieces
1 ounce chorizo, chopped
1 onion, finely chopped
2 celery stalks, chopped
1 green bell pepper, seeded and chopped
1 red bell pepper, seeded and chopped
2 garlic cloves, crushed
1 fresh green chili, seeded and finely chopped
1 fresh red chili, seeded and finely chopped
1¼ cups canned diced tomatoes
1 tablespoon chili paste
2 cups reduced-sodium chicken broth
1 cup brown long-grain rice (preferably basmati)
7 ounces raw peeled shrimp
pepper, to taste
2 tablespoons chopped fresh flat-leaf parsley, to garnish

1. Heat the oil in a large skillet with a lid over medium-high heat, then add the chicken and cook, uncovered, for 1–2 minutes. Add the chorizo and cook for another minute, stirring, until it begins to release its oils. Using a slotted spoon, remove the chicken and chorizo from the pan and set aside.

2. Reduce the heat to medium-low, stir the onion, celery, green bell pepper, and red bell pepper into the pan and cook for 5–10 minutes, until soft, adding a little of the broth if the pan gets dry.

3. Add the garlic to the pan with the chilies. Cook for 1 minute, then stir in the tomatoes, chili paste, and a little of the broth, season with pepper, and cook for an additional minute.

4. Stir in most of the remaining broth and the rice. Bring to a simmer, return the chicken and chorizo to the pan, and cook, covered and without stirring, for 16 minutes. Lift the lid to check that the dish isn't too dry. If it is, stir in the remaining broth or a little boiling water, cover, and cook for an additional 4 minutes. If it is too wet, remove the lid for the rest of the cooking time. Stir in the shrimp to cook through for the last 3 minutes of the cooking time. The paella is ready when the rice has absorbed almost all of the broth and is tender, and the chicken, shrimp, and vegetables are cooked through.

5. Garnish with parsley and serve immediately.

Serves: 4 / / Preparation time: 25 minutes / / Cooking time: 35–40 minutes

Basmati rice has a lower GI rating than other types of rice, while brown rice contains more fiber and nutrients than white rice.

1
3
4

Breaded Fish with Chunky Fries

This version of the popular fish and chips dish tastes fantastic and is much lower in calories, fat, and sodium, because it is all cooked in the oven.

Calories 412 / / Carbohydrates 54.9 g / / Sugars 7.2 g / / Protein 35.2 g / / Fiber 8.4 g / / Fat 9.8 g / / Saturated fat 1.6 g / / Sodium 600 mg

1 egg, beaten
⅔ cup dried whole-wheat bread crumbs
2 teaspoons low-sodium season-all seasoning
4 skinless cod loin fillets (about 5 ounces each)
4 large floury potatoes (about 1 pound 5 ounces), scrubbed and cut into chunky sticks
1 teaspoon garam masala
1 teaspoon paprika
½ teaspoon salt
1 tablespoon peanut oil
cooking spray, for oiling
2 cups frozen peas

Sauce
2 tablespoons light mayonnaise
1 tablespoon fat-free Greek-style yogurt
2 teaspoons lemon juice

1. Preheat the oven to 400°F. Put the beaten egg in a shallow dish. Put the bread crumbs in a separate shallow dish and thoroughly stir in the season-all seasoning. Dry the fish fillets on paper towels.

2. Dry the potato sticks on paper towels. Put them into a large bowl and stir in the garam masala, paprika, salt, and oil. Combine thoroughly, then spread out the potatoes on a baking sheet. Bake on the top shelf of the preheated oven for 5 minutes.

3. Meanwhile, coat each fish fillet, first in the beaten egg, allowing any excess to drip back into the dish, and then in the bread crumbs. Put them onto a separate baking sheet lined with parchment paper and spray thoroughly with cooking spray.

4. Put the fish in the oven on the shelf beneath the potatoes and bake for 5 minutes. Turn the potatoes over with a large spatula and return to the oven for an additional 10 minutes, or until the potatoes are crisp on the outside and soft in the center and the fish is cooked through.

5. Meanwhile, bring a small saucepan of water to a boil, add the peas, and cook for 5 minutes, or until tender. Drain and keep warm.

6. To make the sauce, combine the mayonnaise, yogurt, and lemon juice in a small bowl.

7. Serve the fish and fries immediately with the peas and sauce.

Serves: 4 / / Preparation time: 20 minutes / / Cooking time: 20 minutes

When choosing potatoes for the fries, try to select a variety that will be soft and floury in the center and crisp and golden on the outside—russets and purple potatoes are both good choices.

2
3
5

1
2
4

Monkfish, Mushroom, and Red Pepper Skewers

Monkfish is firm, meaty, and a perfect fish for kebabs. It also goes extremely well with bacon, so this dish is bound to become a favorite.

Calories 429 // Carbohydrates 41.0 g // Sugars 6.0 g // Protein 40.7 g // Fiber 3.8 g // Fat 12.2 g // Saturated fat 2.6 g // Sodium 680 mg

1 cup brown long-grain rice (preferably basmati)
14 ounces small cremini mushrooms, stems removed
1 pound 7 ounces monkfish tail fillet, or swordfish or red snapper, cut into 1-inch cubes
1 large red bell pepper, seeded and cut into 1-inch squares
3 low-sodium lean bacon slices, trimmed and cut into 1-inch squares
1½ tablespoons olive oil
salt, to taste
fresh cilantro sprigs, to garnish

Sauce
5 pieces semi-dried tomato, finely chopped
1 tablespoon lemon juice
1 large tomato, peeled and finely chopped
1 heaping teaspoon smoked paprika
1 garlic clove, crushed

1. Put the rice into a saucepan of lightly salted water, then cover and cook over low heat for 20 minutes, or until tender.

2. Meanwhile, cut any large mushrooms in half. Thread the fish, mushrooms, red bell pepper, and bacon evenly onto four metal skewers.

3. Preheat the broiler and brush the kebabs with the oil. Place the kebabs on a rack under the preheated broiler and cook for about 4 minutes on each side, or until the fish and bacon are cooked all the way through and the vegetables are tender.

4. To make the sauce, combine the semi-dried tomatoes, lemon juice, tomato, paprika, and garlic in a small bowl.

5. Drain the rice. Serve the kebabs with the rice and a spoonful of the sauce. Garnish with cilantro sprigs.

Serves: 4 // Preparation time: 15 minutes // Cooking time: 25 minutes

If you can't get hold of semi-dried tomatoes, replace them with sun-dried tomatoes in oil.

Salmon Ramen

In this Asian-inspired dish, heart-healthy salmon is given a sticky teriyaki glaze and served in an aromatic broth with noodles and vegetables.

Calories 397 // Carbohydrates 32.7 g // Sugars 4.2 g // Protein 34.2 g // Fiber 2.5 g // Fat 12.4 g // Saturated fat 2.3 g // Sodium 1,200 mg

1. Preheat the broiler to high. Put the broth into a saucepan, add the garlic clove and soy sauce, and bring to a boil.

2. Mix together the ingredients for the glaze and brush one surface of each salmon fillet with the glaze. Lightly brush the broiler rack with the oil and cook the salmon under the preheated broiler for 4 minutes on only one side. The flesh should flake easily, and the center should remain a bright pink. Remove the fish from the broiler and set aside.

3. Cook the noodles according to the package directions. Drain and set aside.

4. Remove the garlic from the broth, then bring the broth back to a boil. Drop in the spinach and scallions and cook until the spinach is just wilted. Use a slotted spoon to remove the spinach and scallions from the pan and divide them among warm bowls. Divide the noodles among the bowls, then add a salmon fillet to each. Carefully pour the boiling broth into each bowl.

5. Sprinkle with the bean sprouts, chili slices, and cilantro sprigs and serve immediately.

Serves: 4 // Preparation time: 15–20 minutes // Cooking time: 20 minutes

3¾ cups reduced-sodium vegetable broth
1 large garlic clove
½ teaspoon light soy sauce
4 skinless salmon fillets (about 5 ounces each)
1½ teaspoons peanut oil
5 ounces dried fine egg noodles or ramen noodles
3½ cups baby spinach
4 scallions, chopped

Glaze
2½ tablespoons sake
2½ tablespoons light soy sauce
2 tablespoons mirin or sweet sherry
1 teaspoon maple syrup
½ garlic clove, finely chopped
¼-inch piece fresh ginger, finely chopped

To Serve
1 cup fresh bean sprouts
1 fresh green chili, seeded and sliced
fresh cilantro sprigs

Salmon is rich in the health-promoting fatty acid DHA (short for docosahexaenoic acid), which can help to reduce the health complications of diabetes.

Tuna and Broccoli Pasta Casserole

Many tuna pasta casserole recipes are high in saturates, sodium, and calories. Not so this version, which is also high in fiber and protein.

Calories 533 // Carbohydrates 54.0 g // Sugars 10.1 g //Protein 32.0 g // Fiber 8.1 g // Fat 19.7 g // Saturated fat 5.7 g // Sodium 640 mg

8½ ounces dried whole-wheat penne pasta
3 cups broccoli florets
1 (12-ounce) can solid white tuna in olive oil, drained and 1½ tablespoons of the oil reserved
1 tablespoon red pesto
1½ cups tomato puree or sauce with onions and garlic
6 cherry tomatoes, halved
½ cup reduced-fat cream cheese
½ cup shredded reduced-fat cheddar or American cheese
½ cup fresh whole-wheat bread crumbs
salt, to taste
7 cups mixed salad greens, to serve

1. Preheat the oven to 375°F. Bring a large saucepan of lightly salted water to a boil, then add the pasta and cook for 10–12 minutes, or according to package directions, until tender but still firm to the bite. Drain.

2. Meanwhile, steam the broccoli florets until just tender. Flake the tuna.

3. Put the tuna oil, pesto, and tomato puree or sauce into a saucepan and cook, stirring, over medium-high heat for 1–2 minutes, until warmed through.

4. Put the cooked pasta into a shallow ovenproof dish along with the sauce, broccoli, cherry tomatoes, and tuna. Stir gently to make sure all the pasta is well covered.

5. Dot the top with the cream cheese, then sprinkle with the shredded cheese and bread crumbs. Bake in the preheated oven for 20 minutes, or until heated through and the cheese is golden and melted. Serve immediately with the salad greens.

Serves: 4 // Preparation time: 15 minutes // Cooking time: 35 minutes

Broccoli has anti-inflammatory properties, and is a rich source of vitamin C. Steamed broccoli has a more marked ability to lower blood cholesterol than broccoli cooked in any other way.

1
3
5

1
3
4

Lentil Burgers

The whole family—whether vegetarian or not—will enjoy these burgers made from tasty green lentils threaded through with green spinach.

Calories 363 / / Carbohydrates 47.5 g / / Sugars 4.4 g / / Protein 18.0 g / / Fiber 11.2 g / / Fat 12.6 g / / Saturated fat 2.1 g / / Sodium 880 mg

1. Bring a small saucepan of lightly salted water to a boil, add the potato, and cook for 10 minutes, until soft. Drain thoroughly, then return to the stove with the heat turned off. The residual heat will dry out any remaining moisture—shake the pan to help.

2. Meanwhile, put the spinach in a microwave-safe bowl and microwave at full power (850 watts) for 1½ minutes, or until thoroughly wilted. Transfer to a strainer and push all the moisture out using the end of a rolling pin or a pestle. Dry again on strong paper towels.

3. Put the potato, lentils, onion, mushrooms, 1 teaspoon of salt, and pepper to taste in a food processor and process for 1 minute to a semi-smooth mixture with some texture. Stir the spinach, parsley, and thyme into the mixture by hand, then stir in the egg. Shape into four large ½-inch thick patties.

4. Heat the oil in a large, nonstick skillet. Add the burgers and cook, in batches, if necessary, over medium heat for 3 minutes on each side. You may need to reduce the heat to low for the last minute of cooking on each side to prevent the burgers from overbrowning.

5. Halve the burger buns and spread them with the mayonnaise. Place the patties in the buns with the tomato slices and serve immediately with the salad greens on the side.

Serves: 4 / / Preparation time: 20 minutes / / Cooking time: 25 minutes

- 1 russet or other floury potato (about 3½ ounces), cut into ¾-inch cubes
- 3½ cups baby spinach
- 2¼ cups cooked green lentils
- 1 onion, coarsely chopped
- 1½ cups coarsely chopped cremini mushrooms
- 1 heaping tablespoon chopped fresh parsley
- 2 teaspoons fresh thyme leaves
- 1 medium egg, beaten
- 1½ tablespoons canola oil
- 1 tsp salt
- pepper, to taste

To Serve

- 4 whole-wheat burger buns, about 1¾ ounces each
- ¼ cup light mayonnaise
- 1 large tomato, sliced
- 1 (8-ounce) package mixed salad greens

When choosing a bag of mixed salad greens to serve with this burger, try to buy one with a good variety of deep-colored leaves in it, such as dark green, purple, or red—these leaves contain the most nutrients and antioxidants.

Butternut Squash and Spinach Curry

Squash makes a delightful main ingredient for a curry and goes particularly well with coconut milk in this easy dinner.

Calories 486 / / Carbohydrates 80.2 g / / Sugars 8.8 g / / Protein 11.7 g / / Fiber 10.6 g / / Fat 14.1 g / / Saturated fat 5.9 g / / Sodium 680 mg

Butternut and other winter squashes are an especially useful food for diabetics because they contain the compound inositol and the fiber pectin, both of which help to regulate blood sugar and insulin production.

- 1 tablespoon peanut oil
- 1 large onion, sliced
- 2 garlic cloves, crushed
- 1¼-inch piece fresh ginger, finely chopped
- ¼ cup korma curry paste
- 1 small butternut squash, peeled, seeded, and cut into bite-size cubes (about 15 ounces prepared weight)
- 1 (15-ounce) can chickpeas, drained and rinsed
- 1¼ cups light coconut milk
- 2 cups water
- ½ teaspoon salt
- 1 cup brown long-grain rice (preferably basmati)
- 7 cups fresh spinach
- large handful of fresh cilantro leaves

1. Heat the oil in a large saucepan, then add the onion and cook over medium-low heat for 5 minutes, or until soft. Add the garlic and ginger and cook, stirring, for 1 minute.

2. Increase the heat to medium-high, add the curry paste, and cook for 2 minutes. Add the squash, chickpeas, and coconut milk, stir well, and bring to a simmer. Reduce the heat to low and simmer for 25 minutes, or until the squash is tender.

3. Meanwhile, put the water into a saucepan with the salt, cover, and bring to a simmer. Add the rice and simmer for 25 minutes, or according to package directions, until the rice is tender and the water has been absorbed.

4. Stir the spinach into the curry and let it wilt for 1 minute. Sprinkle the cilantro leaves over the curry and serve immediately with the rice.

Serves: 4 / / Preparation time: 15–20 minutes / / Cooking time: 35–40 minutes

Winter Root Vegetable Casserole

This spicy casserole is a good option for a meat-free meal. Its huge fiber content makes it extremely satisfying, and it is also low in saturates.

Calories 458 / / Carbohydrates 81 g / / Sugars 11.5 g / / Protein 13.7 g / / Fiber 11.6 g / / Fat 9 g / / Saturated fat 1.4 g / / Sodium 840 mg

1 tablespoon olive oil
2 red onions, thickly sliced
2 large garlic cloves, crushed
2 tablespoons tomato paste
2 tablespoons harissa paste
2 carrots, cut into thick sticks
1 Yukon Gold potato (about 3½ ounces), cut into 1¼-inch chunks
1 large sweet potato (about 7 ounces), cut into 1¼-inch chunks
½ rutabaga (about 7 ounces), cut into ½-inch thick circles, then quartered, or 1½ cups diced butternut squash
2½ cups reduced-sodium vegetable broth
1 cup cooked lima beans or cannellini beans
1¼ cups canned diced tomatoes
pinch of salt (optional)
1 cup whole-wheat couscous
large handful of fresh flat-leaf parsley, chopped
pepper, to taste

1. Heat the oil in a flameproof casserole dish, add the onions, and cook over medium-low heat for 5 minutes, or until soft and transparent. Add the garlic, tomato paste, and harissa paste and cook, stirring, for 1 minute.

2. Add the carrots, potato, sweet potato, and rutabaga or squash. Pour in the broth, season with pepper, and bring to a simmer. Cover and cook for 30 minutes, or until the vegetables are almost soft, stirring once halfway through.

3. Stir in the beans and tomatoes and cook for an additional 15 minutes. Press some of the beans into the side of the casserole dish to break them up and thicken the sauce. Check the seasoning, adding more pepper, if desired, and a pinch of salt, if using.

4. Meanwhile, prepare the couscous according to the package directions.

5. Sprinkle the parsley over the casserole and serve immediately with the couscous.

Serves: 4 / / Preparation time: 25 minutes / / Cooking time: 1 hour

Orange and yellow vegetables, such as carrots, sweet potatoes, and rutabaga, are rich in beta-carotene, which can help reduce the risk of coronary heart disease. Sweet potatoes also have a lower GI rating than standard potatoes.

Sides and Snacks

Sweet Potato Fries

Orange-fleshed sweet potatoes make a simple and tasty alternative to regular fries in this delicious, low-fat recipe.

Calories 183 / / Carbohydrates 35.7 g / / Sugars 7.0 g / / Protein 2.9 g / / Fiber 5.3 g / / Fat 3.5 g / / Saturated fat 0.5 g / / Sodium 400 mg

Sweet potatoes are worth choosing over regular potatoes at least some of the time because they offer several additional benefits for your health. They are richer in vitamins C and A, and they also contain more fiber.

1 tablespoon peanut oil
4 small sweet potatoes (about 1½ pounds)
½ teaspoon salt
½ teaspoon ground cumin
¼ teaspoon cayenne pepper

1. Preheat the oven to 450°F. Brush a large baking sheet with a little of the oil.

2. Peel the sweet potatoes and slice into ¼-inch-thick spears about 3 inches long. Spread the sweet potatoes on the prepared baking sheet, pour over the remaining oil, and toss to coat.

3. In a small bowl, combine the salt, cumin, and cayenne pepper. Sprinkle the spice mixture evenly over the sweet potatoes and then toss again.

4. Spread the sweet potatoes out into a single layer and bake in the preheated oven for 15–20 minutes, or until cooked through and lightly colored. Serve hot.

Serves: 4 / / Preparation time: 10 minutes / / Cooking time: 15–20 minutes

Crushed Celery Root and New Potatoes

Try this rustic side as an accompaniment to a food high in protein, such as lean venison sausages, roasted chicken, or lamb cutlets.

Calories 144 // Carbohydrates 25.0 g // Sugars 2.8 g // Protein 3.2 g // Fiber 4.2 g // Fat 3.9 g // Saturated fat 0.6 g // Sodium 360 mg

Celery root has a high GI rating, but the addition of the skin-on new potatoes and oil, and the fact that you don't completely mash the vegetables, means that this dish has a medium glycemic load overall.

1 small celery root (about 14 ounces), peeled and cut into ¾-inch chunks
14 ounces new potatoes, scrubbed and cut into ¾-inch chunks
2 garlic cloves, crushed
1 tablespoon olive oil
½ cup reduced-sodium vegetable broth
½ teaspoon celery salt
2 teaspoons fresh thyme leaves
1 tablespoon chopped fresh flat-leaf parsley
pepper, to taste

1. Put the celery root into a large skillet over medium-high heat. Add the potatoes, garlic, and oil and stir. Sauté for 3–4 minutes, stirring occasionally, until the vegetables are lightly browned.

2. Pour in the broth, add the celery salt and thyme, season with pepper, and bring to a simmer. Cover and braise the vegetables for 20 minutes, adding a little water if they begin to look dry.

3. Using a potato masher, bang the vegetables in the pan—don't mash them; just break them down into smallish pieces. Sprinkle with the parsley, stir, and serve immediately.

Serves: 4 // Preparation time: 15 minutes // Cooking time: 25 minutes

1
2
3

1
2
3

Roasted Onion and Winter Root Vegetables

For a healthy alternative to roasted potatoes, this mixed vegetable side complements any roasted meat, particularly beef and chicken.

Calories 252 // Carbohydrates 50.6 g // Sugars 11.0 g // Protein 4.7 g // Fiber 8.1 g // Fat 3.8 g // Saturated fat 0.2 g // Sodium 520 mg

2 red onions, quartered
6 small shallots
2 parsnips, cut into thick sticks
1 large sweet potato (about 7 ounces), cut into thick sticks
7 ounces yam, cut into thick sticks (about 1⅓ cups)
5½ ounces Jerusalem artichokes, scrubbed and halved (about 1 cup)
8 large garlic cloves, unpeeled
1 tablespoon canola oil
1 tablespoon lemon juice
1 teaspoon salt
pepper, to taste

1. Preheat the oven to 375°F. Put the onions and shallots into a roasting pan.

2. Add the parsnips, sweet potato, yam, Jerusalem artichokes, and garlic to the roasting pan.

3. Pour in the oil and lemon juice. Season with the salt and pepper, then stir so that the vegetables are thoroughly coated with the oil and lemon juice.

4. Bake in the preheated oven for 20 minutes. Turn the vegetables with a spatula and bake for an additional 25 minutes, or until they are golden brown and cooked through. The garlic cloves should be meltingly soft inside—if you want, press the flesh of each garlic clove out and into the pan juices and stir in with a little water. Serve immediately.

Serves: 4 // Preparation time: 15 minutes // Cooking time: 45 minutes

Onions and many root vegetables are surprisingly high in sugars, but their high fiber content means that these sugars will not cause a sudden spike in your blood sugars. Yams are high in resistant starch.

Avocado, Tomato, Basil, and Red Onion Salad

This simple salad would be great served with almost anything. It could also be turned into a lunch dish with the addition of buffalo mozzarella.

Calories 196 / / Carbohydrates 10.0 g / / Sugars 2.3 g / / Protein 2.1 g / / Fiber 5.8 g / / Fat 17.0 g / / Saturated fat 2.4 g / / Sodium 480 mg

2 ripe avocados, halved and pitted
1 small red onion, thinly sliced
12 cherry tomatoes, halved
handful of fresh basil leaves

Dressing
2 tablespoons extra virgin olive oil
1½ teaspoons red wine vinegar
1 teaspoon balsamic vinegar
1 teaspoon dijon mustard
1 teaspoon salt
1 drop of stevia liquid
pepper, to taste

1. To make the dressing, combine the oil, red wine vinegar, balsamic vinegar, mustard, salt, stevia liquid, and pepper in a small bowl.

2. Holding half an avocado in your palm, insert the tip of a tablespoon into the narrow end of the fruit, and up between the flesh and skin so that the flesh is removed in one piece. Put it onto a board and repeat with the other halves, then cut diagonally into ¼-inch slices. Halve the onion slices.

3. Arrange the avocado slices and cherry tomatoes on a serving plate and sprinkle with the onion pieces. Spoon the dressing over the vegetables and sprinkle the basil on top. Serve immediately.

Serves: 4 / / Preparation time: 10 minutes / / Cooking time: None

This salad is high in fat (albeit the healthy monounsaturated type) so if you are watching your weight, serve it with a low-fat accompaniment to bring down the overall calorie count of the meal.

1
2
3

Red Cabbage, Orange, and Walnut Coleslaw

A refreshing and tangy salad you'll want to make time and again to go with steak, roasted chicken, or anything else you want.

Calories 148 // Carbohydrates 10.2 g // Sugars 4.7 g // Protein 2.7 g // Fiber 3.0 g // Fat 11.7 g // Saturated fat 1.0 g // Sodium 480 mg

1 cup thinly shredded red cabbage
1 cup thinly shredded white cabbage
1 small red onion, thinly sliced
1 orange
⅓ cup walnut pieces
handful of fresh cilantro leaves

Dressing
1½ tablespoons walnut oil
2 teaspoons white wine vinegar
1 teaspoon dijon mustard
1 drop of stevia liquid
½ teaspoon salt
pepper, to taste

1. Put the red cabbage and white cabbage into a serving bowl.

2. Halve the onion slices and add to the bowl.

3. Using a sharp knife, cut a slice from the top and the bottom of the orange. Remove the peel and white pith by cutting downward, following the shape of the fruit as closely as possible. Working over a small bowl to catch any juice, cut between the flesh and the membrane of each segment and ease out the flesh. Slice each segment in half. Squeeze the membrane over a small bowl to extract the juice. Add the orange pieces to the serving bowl.

4. To make the dressing, add the oil, vinegar, mustard, stevia liquid, salt, and pepper to the bowl with the orange juice and whisk together.

5. Stir the dressing, walnut pieces, and cilantro into the serving bowl. Serve immediately.

Serves: 4 // Preparation time: 15 minutes // Cooking time: None

Cabbage has a low GI rating of about 15, so it's an ideal vegetable to include in your diet. The addition of oil-rich walnuts and walnut oil helps slow down the rate at which the food is absorbed into your bloodstream.

1
3
4

Fresh Caribbean Salsa

Here is a salad to perk up your taste buds—try serving it with ham or spicy chicken, or stir some shrimp or crab into it for a simple appetizer.

Calories 74 // Carbohydrates 10.0 g // Sugars 5.5 g // Protein 1.2 g // Fiber 1.7 g // Fat 3.7 g // Saturated fat 0.2 g // Sodium 80 mg

1 large yellow bell pepper, seeded and cut into ½-inch dice
½ cucumber, quartered, seeded, and cut into ½-inch dice
2 slices fresh pineapple, about ½-inch thick, chopped
2 scallions, chopped
2 fresh red chilies, seeded and finely chopped
handful of fresh cilantro leaves, to garnish

Dressing
juice of 1 lime
1 teaspoon jerk seasoning
1 tablespoon extra virgin canola oil

1. Put the yellow bell pepper, cucumber, pineapple, scallions, and chilies into a serving bowl.

2. To make the dressing, combine the lime juice, jerk seasoning, and oil in a small bowl.

3. Pour the dressing over the salad and stir thoroughly. Sprinkle the cilantro over the top and serve immediately.

Serves: 4 // Preparation time: 15 minutes // Cooking time: None

Regular consumption of (unpeeled) cucumber is excellent for anyone who has hypertension, which can lead to heart disease. This is because it is high in potassium, which can significantly lower blood pressure.

Cannellini Bean Dip with Crudités

Try this enjoyable dip, served with crunchy raw vegetables and strips of pita bread. It makes a good appetizer or snack—or even party food.

Calories 184 / / Carbohydrates 19.0 g / / Sugars 2.1 g / / Protein 6.3 g / / Fiber 4.7 g / / Fat 8.6 g / / Saturated fat 1.2 g / / Sodium 520 mg

Small cannellini (white kidney) beans are high in resistant starch, as well as being high in both soluble and insoluble fibers, so this dip is one of the best snacks you can eat to help control blood sugars.

1 whole-wheat pita bread
⅓ cucumber, quartered lengthwise, seeded, and cut into sticks
3 celery stalks, halved lengthwise and cut into sticks
4 radishes, quartered

Dip
1 (15-ounce) can cannellini beans in water, drained and rinsed
3 garlic cloves, crushed
juice of ½ lemon
2½ tablespoons olive oil
1 teaspoon salt
pepper, to taste

1. To make the dip, put the beans into the bowl of a food processor. Add the garlic, lemon juice, oil, salt, and pepper. Pulse for 20 seconds, or until a thick paste forms. Alternatively, put the ingredients into a mixing bowl and beat thoroughly with a wooden spoon to combine. Add a little water if the mixture is too stiff. Transfer to a small bowl.

2. Lightly toast the pita bread and cut into eight strips.

3. Place the bowl of dip in the center of a plate, surrounded by the crudités and pita bread strips. Serve immediately.

Serves: 4 / / Preparation time: 15 minutes / / Cooking time: 5 minutes

1
1
1

2
3
6

Mixed Vegetable Chips

These chips—made with a combination of root vegetables—are even more delicious than the higher-GI ones you can buy at the supermarket.

Calories 128 / / Carbohydrates 19.2 g / / Sugars 5.4 g / / Protein 1.8 g / / Fiber 4.1 g / / Fat 5.2 g / / Saturated fat 0.7 g / / Sodium 520 mg

2 carrots (about 3½ ounces)
1 parsnip (about 3½ ounces)
1 small sweet potato (about 3½ ounces)
2 fresh beets (about 3½ ounces)
4½ ounces new potatoes, unpeeled
1½ tablespoons olive oil
1 teaspoon salt
½ teaspoon sweet paprika
pepper, to taste

1. Preheat the oven to 375°F. Line three baking sheets with parchment paper.

2. Thinly slice the carrots, parsnip, sweet potato, beets, and potatoes. (If possible, use a mandoline or other adjustable-blade slicer or a food processor to do this so that the slices are especially thin.)

3. Dry the vegetable slices between sheets of thick paper towels.

4. Combine the oil with the salt, paprika, and pepper in a small bowl. Put all the vegetables except the beets into a large bowl and add most of the oil mixture—toss thoroughly to combine.

5. Put the beets into a separate bowl with the remaining oil mixture and toss well. (If you toss the beets with the other vegetables, their color will bleed into them.)

6. Arrange the vegetable slices on the prepared baking sheets, keeping the beets separate. Bake in the center of the preheated oven for 10 minutes, then turn the vegetables with a spatula and bake for an additional 5–10 minutes, or until they are golden and cooked through.

7. Transfer to wire racks and let cool until crisp. Toss all the vegetable chips to combine before transferring to a bowl to serve.

Serves: 4 / / Preparation time: 15–20 minutes / / Cooking time: 15–20 minutes, plus cooling

Baking or roasting root vegetables helps to increase their levels of resistant starch.

Homemade Cashew Butter

Making your own nut butter is easy, and unlike many store-bought nut butters, this one is free of added sugar.

Calories 153 // Carbohydrates 8.4 g // Sugars 1.6 g // Protein 5.0 g // Fiber 0.9 g // Fat 12.0 g // Saturated fat 2.1 g // Sodium 120 mg

1 pound 2 ounces whole raw cashew nuts
1 teaspoon salt
½ teaspoon vanilla extract

1. Preheat the oven to 275°F. Put the nuts into the bowl of a food processor with the salt. Grind to small pieces. Process, taking a rest every minute or so, until the nuts warm up and begin to release their oils.

2. Continue processing until a creamy, silky nut butter forms. Add the vanilla extract and process once more to combine.

3. Wash two 8-ounce screw-top jars and rinse thoroughly, then dry with a clean dish towel or paper towels. Put the jars on a baking sheet and heat in the preheated oven for 20 minutes. Sterilize the lids by boiling them in water for 5 minutes, then dry them on paper towels.

4. Using a clean spoon, fill the jars with the nut butter and cover with the lids. Store in the refrigerator to preserve the unsaturated oils in the butter. Remove from the refrigerator 1 hour before using so the butter will spread more easily. It will keep in the refrigerator for several weeks.

Makes: 18 servings (each 1 heaping tablespoon/ 1 ounce) // Preparation time: 15 minutes // Cooking time: 20 minutes (to sterilize jars)

Buy whole cashew nuts for this recipe (instead of cashew nut pieces), because they will have retained more of their valuable unsaturated fats. Don't use roasted nuts; otherwise, the recipe won't work.

Fruit, Nut, and Seed Trail Mix

This trail mix is lower in sugars than many store-bought mixes. It's worth keeping a small container with you to nibble on during the day.

Calories 132 // Carbohydrates 7.5 g // Sugars 3.0 g // Protein 4.5 g // Fiber 2.4 g // Fat 10.4 g // Saturated fat 1.5 g // Sodium Trace

2¼ cups almonds
3 tablespoons pine nuts
3 tablespoons pumpkin seeds
3 tablespoons sunflower seeds
⅔ cup dried banana chips
2 dates, pitted and coarsely chopped
2 tablespoons oat bran
½ teaspoon ground allspice
1 medium egg white

1. Preheat the oven to 400°F. Combine the almonds, pine nuts, pumpkin and sunflower seeds, banana chips, dates, oat bran, and allspice in a large bowl and mix well.

2. Lightly beat the egg white with a fork in a small bowl, then add to the nut mixture in the bowl, stirring to coat all the ingredients evenly.

3. Spread the mixture out in a single layer on a large baking sheet. Bake in the preheated oven for 8–10 minutes, or until crisp and lightly browned.

4. Let cool completely before serving. The trail mix will keep for up to five days stored in an airtight container.

Makes: 17 servings (each 2½ tablespoons / 1 ounce) // Preparation time: 10 minutes // Cooking time: 8–10 minutes, plus cooling

Eating just a small handful of almonds a day provides a host of health benefits. Almonds have been shown to aid weight loss and reduce abdominal fat. They can also help to prevent hunger and moderate blood glucose levels in diabetics.

1
2
3

Simple Snacks

The ideal snack is one that has a good balance of carbohydrates and protein; contains a little—but not too much—fat (unless it is mostly healthy monounsaturated or Omega-3 fats); contains some vitamins and minerals; has a good fiber content; and is low in sugar. Here are some ideas that will all contribute to a healthy diet and help to keep your blood sugar on an even keel until your next meal, without offering too many calories. You can freely add salad greens, cucumber, radish, and fresh herbs to your choice of snack.

TIP: *Try to balance your choice of snack with what you ate during the previous meal and will be eating at the next one. For example, if your next meal will be high in fresh vegetables, it is fine if your snack is just cheese and a cracker.*

1 hard-boiled egg with a dark rye crispbread
(Calories 114 / Carbohydrates 6.7 g)

*

1 slice reduced-salt ham spread with a little dijon mustard and rolled up in a lettuce leaf
(Calories 36 / Carbohydrates 1.0 g)

*

Small handful (about 3 tbsp./¾ ounce) of almonds
(Calories 115 / Carbohydrates 4.3 g)

*

Small handful of any seeds with 2 dried apricots
(Calories 101 / Carbohydrates 6.0 g)

*

¾-inch square reduced-fat cheddar cheese with 1 oat cake and a cherry tomato
(Calories 109 / Carbohydrates 7.1 g)

*

1 tbsp. hummus with ½ whole-wheat pita bread
(Calories 102 / Carbohydrates 16.4 g)

*

1 tbsp. peanut or cashew nut butter on 1 celery stalk
(Calories 100 / Carbohydrates 4.6 g)

*

1 tbsp. guacamole with ½ slice (about ½ ounce) dark rye bread
(Calories 113 / Carbohydrates 7.2 g)

*

1 carrot cut into sticks and served with 1½ tbsp. tzatziki cucumber yogurt dip
(Calories 84 / Carbohydrates 7.8 g)

*

½ cup plain yogurt with 1 tbsp. milled flaxseed and 1 tsp. agave nectar
(Calories 133 / Carbohydrates 13.1 g)

*

½ whole-wheat English muffin with 1 tbsp. extra-light cream cheese and tomato slices
(Calories 97 / Carbohydrates 14.8 g)

*

2 ½ tbsp./1 ounce of *Fruit, nut, and seed trail mix* (see page 130)
(Calories 132 / Carbohydrates 7.5 g)

Baking and Desserts

1
2
5

Pumpernickel Bread

This unusual recipe for a dark rye loaf contains grits, potatoes, and cocoa. The result is a rich, dark, and flavorsome bread.

Calories 135 / / Carbohydrates 27.8 g / / Sugars 3.7 g / / Protein 5.0 g / / Fiber 6.2 g / / Fat 1.5 g / / Saturated fat 0.2 g / / Sodium 160 mg

½ cup quick-cooking grits
1¼ cups cold water
¼ cup firmly packed dark brown sugar
1 tablespoon light olive oil
1½ teaspoons salt
2 teaspoons caraway seeds
1 tablespoon unsweetened cocoa powder
1 cup cold or lukewarm mashed potatoes
3 cups plus 2 tablespoons dark rye flour
1¼ cups whole-wheat flour, plus extra for sprinkling
4½ teaspoons active dry yeast
½ cup lukewarm water
cooking spray, for oiling

1. Put the grits into a saucepan with the cold water and cook over low heat, stirring constantly, for 5 minutes, or according to package directions, until it has thickened to an oatmeal-like consistency. Remove from the heat and add the sugar, oil, salt, caraway seeds, and cocoa powder. Stir to combine and let cool slightly.

2. Stir in the mashed potatoes, then add the rye flour, whole-wheat flour, yeast, and lukewarm water and knead for 10 minutes, or until the dough is smooth and pliable.

3. Spray a large bowl with cooking spray and put the dough in the bowl. Cover with a clean dish towel and let stand in a warm place for about 45 minutes, or until doubled in size.

4. Meanwhile, preheat the oven to 375°F. Spray a 9-inch loaf pan with cooking spray.

5. Put the dough into the prepared pan, shaping it to fit. Make a few diagonal cuts along the top and sprinkle with a little whole-wheat flour. Bake in the preheated oven for 1 hour, or until the loaf sounds hollow when tapped on the bottom. Let cool in the pan for 10 minutes, then transfer to a wire rack to cool completely.

Makes: 20 slices / / Preparation time: 25–30 minutes, plus rising / / Cooking time: 1 hr 10 mins, plus cooling

The dark rye flour and cocoa bring the glycemic load of this bread right down so that you can enjoy a slice knowing that your blood sugars are not going to suddenly spike.

Cheese and Herb Biscuits

These delicious cheese biscuits are an excellent midmorning treat, or you could try one instead of bread with soup for lunch.

Calories 213 / / Carbohydrates 32.0 g / / Sugars 1.1 g / / Protein 7.9 g / / Fiber 2.8 g / / Fat 6.4 g / / Saturated fat 2.9 g / / Sodium 480 mg

- cooking spray, for oiling
- 2¾ cups whole-wheat flour
- 2¾ cups all-purpose white flour, plus extra for dusting
- 2 tablespoons baking powder
- ¼ teaspoon salt
- 5½ tablespoons margarine (from a block), chopped
- ¾ cup shredded reduced-fat sharp cheddar cheese
- 1½ tablespoons finely snipped fresh chives
- 1 tablespoon finely chopped fresh rosemary leaves
- 1¼ cups low-fat milk
- ⅓ cup freshly grated Parmesan cheese

1. Preheat the oven to 425°F. Spray a large baking sheet with cooking spray.

2. Sift the whole-wheat flour, all-purpose white flour, baking powder, and salt into a mixing bowl, tipping in any bran left in the sifter, and stir to combine. Add the margarine and rub it into the flour with your fingertips until the mixture resembles bread crumbs. Stir in the cheddar cheese, chives, and rosemary.

3. Make a well in the center of the dry ingredients and pour in all but 2 tablespoons of the milk, stirring with a spatula until a dough begins to form, then finish the process using your hands. If necessary, add a little more milk or water (you need only enough to form a stiff dough).

4. Turn out onto a lightly floured work surface and knead gently to form a smooth dough. Add more flour to the work surface and the rolling pin, if needed, then roll out the dough to ¾-inch thick. Cut out 16 biscuits with a 3-inch round cutter.

5. Put the biscuits on the prepared sheet, evenly spaced out. Brush the tops with the remaining milk, then sprinkle with the Parmesan cheese. Bake in the preheated oven for 15–20 minutes, or until the biscuits are golden, cooked through, and sound hollow when tapped on the bottom. Serve warm or cold. The biscuits can be frozen for up to one month.

Makes: 16 / / Preparation time: 20–25 minutes / / Cooking time: 15–20 minutes, plus cooling

You can use whole-wheat spelt flour instead of the whole-wheat flour for a nutty change. If you want to use self-rising flour instead of the all-purpose white flour, reduce the baking powder to 3¼ teaspoons and omit the salt.

2
2
4

Nut and Seed Bars

The sugar content of many store-bought fruit, nut, and seed bars is often high. These bars bring the sugar down to an acceptable level.

Calories 213 / / Carbohydrates 21.7 g / / Sugars 6.8 g / / Protein 6.2 g / / Fiber 4 g / / Fat 12.0 g / / Saturated fat 1.8 g / / Sodium 120 mg

¼ cup peanut oil
3 tablespoons cashew nut butter (see p. 128)
1 tablespoon maple syrup
2 tablespoons granulated stevia
¼ cup milled flaxseed
1 cup unsweetened applesauce
1 teaspoon vanilla extract
3 cups rolled oats
¾ cup chopped dried apricots
⅓ cup pumpkin seeds
⅓ cup sunflower seeds
½ teaspoon ground cinnamon
¼ teaspoon salt

1. Preheat the oven to 340°F. Line a 9½ x 6¼-inch shallow baking pan with parchment paper.

2. Put the oil, cashew nut butter, maple syrup, and stevia into a small saucepan and heat gently, stirring constantly, until well combined and the nut butter is melted.

3. Remove from the heat, add the flaxseed, applesauce, and vanilla extract and combine thoroughly.

4. Mix together the oats, dried apricots, pumpkin seeds, sunflower seeds, cinnamon, and salt in a large mixing bowl. Spoon the nut butter mixture into the bowl and stir until well combined.

5. Spoon the dough into the prepared pan, pressing it down and out into the corners with your fingers until the pan is evenly filled.

6. Bake in the preheated oven for 40 minutes, or until the top is golden. Let cool in the pan for about 5 minutes, then remove from the pan and cut into 15 bars. Transfer to a wire rack to cool completely. Store in an airtight container for up to one week.

Makes: 15 / / Preparation time: 20 minutes / / Cooking time: 45 minutes, plus cooling

The seed selection in the bars is rich in unsaturated fats—including Omega-3s and monounsaturates—as well as being high in soluble and insoluble fibers and resistant starch.

Oat, Blueberry, and Nut Cookies

Using stevia in this recipe dramatically reduces the total sugar content so that you can enjoy a real fruit and nut cookie without guilt.

Calories 145 / / Carbohydrates 17.0 g / / Sugars 1.4 g / / Protein 3.8 g / / Fiber 2.4 g / / Fat 7.3 g / / Saturated fat 1.4 g / / Sodium 80 mg

- cooking spray, for oiling
- ¼ cup peanut oil
- 4½ tablespoons margarine (from a block), at room temperature
- 3½ tablespoons granulated stevia
- 2 tablespoons honey
- 1 extra-large egg
- 1 teaspoon vanilla extract
- 1¼ cups whole-wheat flour or spelt flour
- ¾ cup all-purpose white flour
- 1¾ cups rolled oats
- ¾ cup steel-cut oats
- 1 teaspoon baking soda
- ¼ teaspoon salt
- 1⅓ cups blueberries
- ¾ cup chopped hazelnuts

1. Preheat the oven to 350°F. Spray a large baking sheet with cooking spray.

2. In a large mixing bowl, beat together the oil, margarine, stevia, and honey until creamy, then beat in the egg and vanilla extract with 1 tablespoon of the flour.

3. In a separate bowl, combine the whole-wheat flour, white flour, rolled oats, steel-cut oats, baking soda, and salt. Add the blueberries and hazelnuts and gently stir to combine (you don't want the blueberries to break up at this stage).

4. Stir the flour mixture into the oil mixture until thoroughly combined. Drop 25 spoonfuls of the dough onto the prepared baking sheet.

5. Bake the cookies in the preheated oven for about 15 minutes, until set around the edges and golden but still with some "give" in the center if you push with your thumb.

6. Using a spatula, transfer the cookies to a wire rack to cool completely. Store in an airtight container for up to one week.

Makes: 25 / / Preparation time: 20–25 minutes / / Cooking time: 15 minutes, plus cooling

Studies on blueberries have shown that they can help with blood sugar control because of the plant compounds (phenols) that they contain.

2

3

4

2
3
4

Pumpkin Pie Muffins

If you love pumpkin pie, the good news is that you can enjoy all those wonderful flavors in a healthy low-fat, low-saturates muffin.

Calories 225 // Carbohydrates 42.0 g // Sugars 7.5 g // Protein 7.6 g // Fiber 5.2 g // Fat 4.1 g // Saturated fat 0.6 g // Sodium 320 mg

1. Preheat the oven to 350°F. Line ten cups in a 12-section muffin pan with muffin cups.

2. Put the flour, oats, baking powder, baking soda, salt, and pumpkin pie spice into a large bowl and mix to combine thoroughly.

3. Beat together the sugar, stevia, egg whites, and vanilla extract in a mixing bowl, then beat in the pumpkin puree, oil, applesauce, and almond milk. Add the flour mixture and beat until just mixed.

4. Divide the batter among the muffin cups. Bake in the preheated oven for 25 minutes, or until a toothpick inserted into the center of a muffin comes out clean.

5. Let the muffins rest in the pan for a few minutes until they are cool enough to handle, then transfer to a wire rack to cool completely. They are best eaten within 24 hours but will store for a little longer, and will freeze for up to one month.

Makes: 10 // Preparation time: 20–25 minutes // Cooking time: 25 minutes, plus cooling

- 2¾ cups whole-wheat flour
- 1½ cups rolled oats
- 1¼ teaspoons baking powder
- ¾ teaspoon baking soda
- ¼ teaspoon salt
- 2 teaspoons ground pumpkin pie spice
- ⅓ cup firmly packed dark brown sugar
- 1 tablespoon granulated stevia
- 2 egg whites
- 2 teaspoons vanilla extract
- 1 cup canned pumpkin puree (not pumpkin pie mix)
- 1½ tablespoons peanut oil
- ⅓ cup unsweetened applesauce
- 1 cup unsweetened vanilla almond milk

To make your own pumpkin puree, put 3 cups pumpkin chunks into a microwave-safe bowl with a little water. Cook in a microwave at 850 watts for 8 minutes, or until tender and soft enough to mash easily, then mash to a puree.

Fitting Your Favorite Foods into Your Diet

There is no food that must be completely banned from your diet, even if you are diabetic. What ultimately matters is the overall quality of your diet, and that you monitor your carbohydrate intake, especially if you are using supplementary insulin. It is always sensible to make sure that at each meal or snack occasion you balance what you eat so that the total glycemic load of the meal is acceptable.

To do this is simple enough. For example, if your favorite food happens to be a high-sugar, low-fiber item, such as candy, then limit how much you eat and add a high-protein/moderate-fat item to the snack to bring down its glycemic load—in this case, you might add a few nuts. This trick also has the benefit of keeping you feeling full for longer and avoiding the urge to dip into the candies later on. To give another example, if you love a plate of white pasta, make sure the topping is a high-protein one with plenty of fiber—for example, tuna and broccoli with peas and tomato sauce.

If you are watching your weight, there are several things you can do to make sure that your favorite foods can be included in your diet without compromising your weight loss or weight maintenance.

* Eat mindfully. Each time you eat a "treat" food or one that you know is high in calories, eat slowly and try to make sure that you really appreciate it, enjoy it, and savor it. When it is finished, feel happy and move away from the food area and do something else that makes you happy.

* It helps to pay full attention to your food at every meal, chewing thoroughly and eating as slowly as you can. By paying attention to what you're doing, you can stop eating the moment you have had enough. This one simple trick can reduce your overall food intake more than you might imagine, so that you then have calories "saved" for a treat.

* Add one or two healthy elements to your favorite meal, if you can, to improve its nutritional profile. For example, if you have a plate of low-fiber white rice and lamb curry, add high-fiber vegetables, such as spinach, broccoli, onions, and tomatoes. This way you may also eat fewer calories and less fat as the vegetables bulk your meal out.

* Limit portion sizes of the foods that are less good for you—it really helps to eat from a smaller plate or dish, and, if cooking, to make a portion in the first place that is not too large, so there are no leftovers to go back for.

* See if you can find a lower-fat, lower-salt, or lower-sugar version of your favorite food that is still acceptable to you. Most supermarkets stock healthier versions of cheese, yogurts, sauces, desserts, chips, prepared meals, and more.

* Try to burn off the calories you eat in a treat through exercise. For example, you choose a chocolate candy bar for a snack. It contains 200 calories. Could you motivate yourself to go for an hour's walk to burn off those calories? You may also find you feel much better about yourself if you do.

* Consider having a set time each day or a day each week to indulge in your favorite food. So 4 p.m. on a workday might be your time for your slice of cake, or Friday evening might be your Italian takeout night. If you know you have a favorite food or meal to look forward to, it can be a positive thing.

* As you begin to eat more healthily in general, don't be surprised to find that you are no longer as interested in the high-sugar, high-salt, or high-saturated fat items you have liked so much in the past. Your taste buds can change—and you may find that you're addicted to all the healthy foods you never thought you'd like.

Beet Brownie Bites

Beets are a valuable baking ingredient, offering bulk, moistness, and sweetness and letting you bake goodies with less sugar and fat.

Calories 74 / / Carbohydrates 7.6 g / / Sugars 4.8 g / / Protein 1.2 g / / Fiber 0.9 g / / Fat 4.4 g / / Saturated fat 1.3 g / / Sodium Trace

cooking spray, for oiling
5½ ounces semisweet chocolate, broken into pieces
2 eggs
1 teaspoon vanilla extract
½ cup firmly packed dark brown sugar
3½ tablespoons granulated stevia
⅓ cup sunflower oil
4 cooked beets (about 8 ounces), shredded
¾ cup whole-wheat flour
¾ teaspoon baking powder
3 tablespoons unsweetened cocoa powder

1. Preheat the oven to 350°F. Spray an 8-inch square cake pan with cooking spray and line with parchment paper.

2. Put the chocolate into a heatproof bowl set over a saucepan of gently simmering water and heat, stirring, until just melted. Remove from the heat.

3. Put the eggs, vanilla extract, brown sugar, and stevia into a large bowl and beat with a handheld electric mixer for 3–4 minutes, or until pale and frothy. Beat in the oil. Stir in the beets, then sift in the flour, baking powder, and cocoa powder, tipping in any bran left in the sifter, and fold in. Add the melted chocolate and stir to combine.

4. Spoon the mixture into the prepared pan, leveling the surface. Bake in the preheated oven for 25–30 minutes, or until just firm to the touch.

5. Let cool in the pan for 5 minutes, then transfer to a wire rack to cool completely. Cut into 36 bite-size squares. Store in an airtight container for up to one week.

Makes: 36 / / Preparation time: 25 minutes / / Cooking time: 30–35 minutes, plus cooling

Beets are a true health food—they can help lower blood pressure and boost stamina, while the plant chemical betaine that they contain is an anti-inflammatory, which can protect your cardiovascular system.

Individual Plum and Rhubarb Crisps

Try one of these fruity crisps—which come in at around 200 calories each—served warm or cold. Either way you eat them, they are delicious.

Calories 208 // Carbohydrates 27.5 g // Sugars 10.6 g // Protein 5.6 g // Fiber 4.2 g // Fat 9.8 g // Saturated fat 1.5 g // Sodium Trace

- 8 ripe sweet plums, halved, pitted, and halved again
- 3 rhubarb stalks, cut into 1-inch lengths (5½ ounces trimmed weight)
- 2 tablespoons granulated stevia
- 1 teaspoon ground cinnamon
- 2 tablespoons water
- 3 tablespoons slivered almonds
- ⅔ cup whole-wheat flour
- 3½ tablespoons margarine (from a block), chilled and cut into small pieces
- ⅓ cup ground almonds
- 2 tablespoons chopped mixed nuts
- 2 tablespoons raw brown sugar
- ¼ cup rolled oats
- ½ cup fresh whole-wheat bread crumbs

1. Preheat the oven to 375°F. Mix the plums and rhubarb with the stevia and cinnamon and put into a microwave-safe dish with the water. Microwave for 3 minutes at 850 watts, or until the fruit has softened but not disintegrated. Alternatively, simmer the fruit mixture gently in a saucepan on the stove for a few minutes.

2. Arrange the fruit in six ¾-cup ramekins (individual ceramic dishes) and stir the slivered almonds evenly into each dish.

3. Sift the flour into a mixing bowl, tipping in any bran left in the sifter. Add the margarine and rub it in with your fingertips until the mixture resembles coarse bread crumbs. Stir in the ground almonds, chopped nuts, sugar, rolled oats, and bread crumbs and mix thoroughly to combine.

4. Divide the crumb mixture evenly among the ramekins, spreading it completely over the top of the fruit. Put the dishes on a baking sheet and bake in the preheated oven for 20–25 minutes, or until the crumb topping is golden and the fruit is bubbling. Let cool for 10 minutes before serving.

Makes: 6 // Preparation time: 25 minutes // Cooking time: 23–28 minutes, plus cooling

Plums are a great fruit to use in desserts if you're watching your sugar intake, because they are naturally sweet but have a low GI rating. The nuts and oats in the topping bring down the total glycemic load of this dessert.

1
2
3

2
4
4

Berry and Bread Puddings

Here's a new take on an old-fashioned favorite—instead of lining a bowl with bread, the bread and fruit are layered in individual dishes.

Calories 224 // Carbohydrates 42.6 g // Sugars 10.5 g // Protein 7.4 g // Fiber 8.0 g // Fat 4.0 g // Saturated fat 0.9 g // Sodium 160 mg

- 1⅔ cups hulled and halved strawberries
- 2 cups raspberries
- ⅔ cup blueberries
- 1 cup red currants (or an extra ½ cup each of raspberries and blueberries)
- 2–3 tablespoons granulated stevia
- 1 tablespoon lemon juice
- 1 teaspoon vanilla extract
- 18 thin slices whole-wheat bread
- 1 cup reduced-fat crème fraîche, quark, or Greek-style yogurt

1. Set aside 12 strawberry halves and 18 raspberries for decoration.

2. Put the remaining berries in a saucepan with the stevia and a little water. Cook over low heat, stirring occasionally, for 8–10 minutes, or until the berries have produced plenty of juice and have broken up a little without completely disintegrating. Remove from the heat and add the lemon juice and vanilla extract.

3. Line six 1-cup ramekins (individual ceramic dishes) with plastic wrap, making sure the plastic is draped over the sides.

4. Cut out a circle the diameter of a ramekin from each slice of bread (the leftover bread can be made into bread crumbs for another recipe) and dip each slice into the fruit saucepan so one side is covered in juice. Use the bread and the berries to layer up each ramekin—first put a little berry juice in the bottom of the ramekin, followed by a bread slice (juice-covered side facing up) and 1–2 spoonfuls of the berries. Repeat the layers until all the berries and bread are used, finishing each dessert with a bread slice on top (juice-covered side facing up).

5. Put the ramekins on a tray and cover the top of each with a small saucer, then place a heavy weight, such as a bag of dried beans, on top of each. Chill in the refrigerator overnight, or until ready to serve.

6. Turn out the desserts onto plates and decorate with the reserved fruit. Top each with a spoonful of the crème fraîche and serve immediately.

Makes: 6 // Preparation time: 25–30 minutes, plus chilling // Cooking time: 8–10 minutes

High-fiber summer berries are an ideal treat. As they need only minimal cooking in this recipe, they retain much of their high levels of vitamin C, which studies suggest may lower the risk of developing type 2 diabetes.

Vanilla Custard Cups with Raspberry Coulis

A creamy custard makes a wonderful dessert, and this vanilla custard is no exception. The tangy berry coulis makes it extra delicious.

Calories 151 // Carbohydrates 17.7 g // Sugars 7.9 g // Protein 6.0 g // Fiber 4.5 g // Fat 6.4 g // Saturated fat 3.0 g // Sodium 80 mg

3¼ cups raspberries
3–4 tablespoons granulated stevia
2–3 tablespoons water
juice of ½ lemon
1 teaspoon arrowroot, if needed
2 eggs
1 teaspoon vanilla extract
2 tablespoons cornstarch
2 cups low-fat milk
1 tablespoon melted butter
1 heaping tablespoon grated semisweet chocolate, to decorate

1. Reserve ¾ cup of the raspberries. Put the remaining raspberries into a microwave-safe bowl with 1 tablespoon of the stevia and the water and cook in the microwave at 850 watts, until the raspberries have disintegrated and there is plenty of juice.

2. Press the raspberries through a strainer into a bowl, using the end of a rolling pin or a pestle to push them through the mesh of the strainer. Stir the lemon juice into the bowl. The mixture should be thicker than juice. If it is too thin, transfer to a small saucepan with the arrowroot and stir over medium heat until thickened. Set aside.

3. Whisk the eggs in a bowl with 2 tablespoons of the remaining stevia and the vanilla extract. Stir in the cornstarch and whisk again until well combined.

4. Heat the milk in a saucepan until just below boiling point. Gradually pour the milk into the egg mixture, whisking constantly, then return the contents of the bowl to the pan.

5. Whisk constantly over medium-low heat until the custard thickens. Remove from the heat and taste it—if it is not quite sweet enough, add more stevia to taste and return to the heat to dissolve it. Whisk in the butter.

6. Spoon the custard into six ⅔-cup glasses and transfer to the refrigerator to cool completely. Top each dessert with some of the raspberry coulis and the reserved raspberries. Sprinkle with the grated chocolate and serve immediately.

Makes: 6 // Preparation time: 15 minutes, plus chilling // Cooking time: 25–30 minutes

You can use other berries for the coulis and topping—try blueberries or blackberries for a change. All berry fruits are rich in vitamin C, fiber, and plant compounds that can help to prevent heart disease.

1
3
5

Fluffy Lemon Whips

These delicious whips use low-calorie, low-fat egg whites to add bulk while lemon gives the flavor and freshness we all love.

Calories 120 / / Carbohydrates 10.8 g / / Sugars 9.5 g / / Protein 10.4 g / / Fiber 0.0 g / / Fat 3.8 g / / Saturated fat 2.5 g / / Sodium 80 mg

Lemons are a source of vitamin C and of the compound limonin, which appears to lower blood cholesterol as well as helping to speed up weight loss.

¼ cup lemon juice
3 tablespoons maple syrup
2 tablespoons granulated stevia
1 fresh mint sprig, plus extra to decorate
4 egg whites
2 teaspoons finely grated lemon zest
1¼ cups Greek-style yogurt

1. Put the lemon juice, maple syrup, stevia, and mint sprig into a small saucepan over high heat and bring to a boil, stirring. Remove from the heat and let stand for 10 minutes.

2. Meanwhile, put the egg whites into a large, grease-free bowl and whisk with a handheld electric mixer until they hold stiff peaks.

3. Remove the mint sprig from the syrup. Add the lemon zest to the syrup, then gradually drizzle the syrup into the beaten egg whites, whisking at high speed. Add the yogurt to the egg white mixture and fold in lightly with a large metal spoon.

4. Spoon into four serving glasses and top each with a mint sprig. Serve immediately.

Serves: 4 / / Preparation time:15 minutes, plus standing / / Cooking time: 5 minutes

1
3
4

Index

This edition published by Cottage Door Press, LLC, in 2019.
First published 2015 by Parragon Books, Ltd.

5005 Newport Drive, Rolling Meadows, Illinois 60008

Author: Judith Wills
Nutritional consultant: Fiona Hunter
Photographer: Mike Cooper
Home economy: Lincoln Jefferson
Designer: Beth Kalynka
Project manager: Louisa Smith
Production controller: Joe Xavier
Images on pages 10, 34–35, 90–91, 133, and 146–147 from Shutterstock.
The cover shows Avocado, Tomato, Basil, and Red Onion Salad (118); Beet Brownie Bites (149); Chicken Scallops with Cherry Tomatoes (88); Smoked Mackerel, Beet, and New Potato Salad (72); Eggplant Paprika Salad (68).

ISBN: 978-1-68052-890-9

Printed in China

Love Food™ is an imprint of Cottage Door Press, LLC.
Parragon Books® and the Parragon® logo are registered trademarks of Cottage Door Press, LLC.

Notes for the Reader

This book uses standard kitchen measuring spoons and cups. All spoon and cup measurements are level unless otherwise indicated. Unless otherwise stated, milk is assumed to be whole, eggs are large, individual vegetables are medium, and pepper is freshly ground black pepper. Unless otherwise stated, all root vegetables should be peeled prior to using. People with nut allergies should be aware that some of the prepared ingredients used in the recipes in this book may contain nuts.

Garnishes, decorations, and serving suggestions are all optional and not necessarily included in the recipe ingredients or method. The times given are only an approximate guide. Preparation times differ according to the techniques used by different people and the cooking times may also vary from those given. Optional ingredients, variations, or serving suggestions have not been included in the time calculations.

While the author has made all reasonable efforts to ensure that the information contained in this book is accurate and up to date at the time of publication, anyone reading this book should note the following important points: Medical and pharmaceutical knowledge is constantly changing and the author and the publisher cannot and do not guarantee the accuracy or appropriateness of the contents of this book; In any event, this book is not intended to be, and should not be relied upon, as a substitute for appropriate, tailored professional advice. Both the author and the publisher strongly recommend that a physician or other healthcare professional is consulted before embarking on major dietary changes; For the reasons set out above, and to the fullest extent permitted by law, the author and publisher: (i) cannot and do not accept any legal duty of care or responsibility in relation to the accuracy or appropriateness of the contents of this book, even where expressed as "advice" or using other words to this effect; and (ii) disclaim any liability, loss, damage, or risk that may be claimed or incurred as a consequence—directly or indirectly—of the use and/or application of any of the contents of this book.